NOT BY ARMS ALONE

LONDON : HUMPHREY MILFORD

OXFORD UNIVERSITY PRESS

NOT BY ARMS ALONE

ESSAYS ON OUR TIME

BY

HANS KOHN

PROFESSOR OF MODERN EUROPEAN HISTORY

SMITH COLLEGE

CAMBRIDGE · MASSACHUSETTS

HARVARD UNIVERSITY PRESS

1941

Second Printing

TO MY STUDENTS
REPRESENTATIVE OF THAT YOUTH
UPON WHOSE RESPONSE
TO THE CHALLENGE OF OUR TIME
THE FUTURE DEPENDS

If we could first know where we are, and whither we are tending, we could better judge what to do, and how to do it.

ABRAHAM LINCOLN, *Speech at Springfield, Illinois, June 16, 1858*

Preface

THE present book is a continuation of my last two books, *Force or Reason* and *Revolutions and Dictatorships*. All three present an attempt at the analysis of our time, as seen against its historical background. In the preface to the third printing of *Force or Reason* I wrote at the beginning of October, 1938: "There is no doubt that there are dark days ahead of us, an age of power politics in which the dignity of the individual and the sanctity of law and truth will count for very little. What we need in such a situation is a clear-sighted and courageous pessimism, free from all illusions, prepared for the worst, but with an unwavering faith in the human values of Western civilization and a determination to stand up for them."

In the two years which have since passed it has become clear to many who did not yet see it in 1938 that we are confronted by the Spenglerian vision of the decline and death of Western civilization. With the realization of the danger, the determination has grown, not to submit to what Spengler regarded and what the Fascists proclaim as inexorable fate, but to stand up for Western civilization with its belief in the equality of men, in the dignity and liberty of the individual, in the brotherhood and common destiny of mankind. Democracy will be able to fulfil this task only if it will revitalize and renovate itself morally, socially and economically. Economic and political forms will change, many of them should change; the fundamental faith of democracy in human values must remain, and must emerge from indifference and cynicism into a living and guiding reality.

In our time the fate of Western civilization and of democracy is being decided — whether we know it or not and whether we wish it or not — everywhere, and in America, for a very long time to come. The struggle is fast developing on a worldwide scale which spans the globe from China and India to the English Channel and to Latin America. We cannot escape it. If we face the facts, if we shake off egotism, fear, and the spirit of defeat, then we shall be able to mobilize all the immense resources of democratic peoples in the Far East, in Europe, and in America, all our intellectual and moral forces, for this final and decisive combat between two incompatible ways of life.

In our time the words with which in 1908 Professor Archibald Cary Coolidge concluded his book *The United States as a World Power* sound prophetic: "The moral for Americans of the various international complications in which they find themselves involved is, after all, the old one that greatness brings responsibilities. . . . They will do well, therefore, to take to heart the words of the President: — 'We have no choice, we people of the United States, as to whether or not we shall play a great part in the world. That has been determined for us by fate, by the march of events. We have to play that part. All that we can decide is whether we shall play it well or ill.' "

Some of the chapters of this book originated in papers read before the American Philosophical Society on November 17, 1939; the American Historical Association, at Washington, D. C., in December 1939; the American Association of University Professors, at Chicago, in December 1938; and the American Association for Adult Education, at New York, in May 1940. They are reprinted here from the *Proceedings of the American Philosophical Society*, vol. lxxxii, no. 1; the *American Scholar*, Summer, 1940; the *Bulletin* of the A.A.U.P., April 1939; and the *Journal of Adult Education*, June 1940, by kind permission of the publishers and editors. The chapters on Central Europe were first published in a somewhat different form in the *Journal of Modern History*, December 1939, and in *Czechoslovakia: Twenty Years of Independence*, edited by Professor Robert J. Kerner. They are reprinted here by kind permission of the University of Chicago Press and the University of California Press. The moving lines by Adam Mickiewicz, translated by Oliver Elton, are quoted from *The Slavonic and Eastern European Review*.

I wish also to express my sincere appreciation of Miss Kathleen Shedd's most efficient help in preparing this volume.

Northampton, Mass.   H. K.
September 1940

Contents

THE TOTALITARIAN
PHILOSOPHY OF WAR

Das Ideal der Sittlichkeit hat keinen gefährlicheren Nebenbuhler als das Ideal der höchsten Stärke, des kräftigsten Lebens, was man auch das Ideal der ästhetischen Grösse benannt hat. Es ist das Maximum der Barbaren und hat leider in diesen Zeiten der verwildernden Kultur gerade unter den grössten Schwächlingen sehr viele Anhänger erhalten. Der Mensch wird durch dieses Ideal zum Tiergeist, eine Vermischung, deren brutaler Witz eben eine brutale Anziehungskraft für Schwächlinge hat.

NOVALIS, *Schriften*, hg. von Tieck
und Schlegel, 2. Teil, S. 266

[There is no greater competitor for the moral ideal than the ideal of supreme strength, of the most powerful life, which ideal has also been called that of esthetic greatness. It is the maxim of the barbarians; unfortunately in these times of cultural bewilderment it has found very many adherents among the greatest weaklings. Through this ideal man becomes an animal-spirit, which mixture, on account of its brutal irony, exercises a brutal attraction upon weaklings.]

The Totalitarian Philosophy of War

CHARACTERISTIC of our time is the progressive disintegration of language as an instrument of universally accepted rational concepts. The same words cover different and sometimes opposite meanings, and much confusion is due to the indiscriminate and ambiguous use of words. One of the words which has lately changed its meaning is "war." Until very recently war was regarded, even by Clausewitz and Bismarck, as a strictly circumscribed and exceptional state of affairs. War was an instrument of politics, to be used only as the *ultima ratio*, as a case *in extremis*. Politics was the art of avoiding war, which was considered an abnormality. The effort of statesmen was concentrated upon maintaining the normal life, and the occurrence of war was frequently regarded as a proof of faulty statesmanship, as a bankruptcy of policy. Even Mussolini ended the article which he contributed under the title "Audacity" to the first issue of his *Il Popolo d'Italia* on November 15, 1914, with the words: "This cry is a word which I would never have used in normal times . . . : a frightening and fascinating word: War!" [1] In the last years, however, Fascism has proclaimed war the normal state of life, not an aberration, caused by an

[1] Benito Mussolini, *Scritti e Discorsi* (Edizione Definitiva, Milan, Ulrico Hoepli), vol. I, p. 10.

intellectual or moral insufficiency, but the culmination in which the vital and ethical energies of man reveal themselves at their best. Politics now becomes a preparation for war, receives its direction and meaning from this extreme *Ernstfall*. War ceases to be anything strictly circumscribed and limited; the border lines between war and peace grow more and more fluid, everything becomes part of warfare, actual or potential, and everything may therefore be called peace. Where the whole way of life is dominated by the norm of war, the words war and peace themselves lose their meaning.

A similar society is known to us from the descriptions of Spartan life in antiquity. This Peloponnesian state, with its economic foundations in the serf labor of the helots and in the exploitation of conquests, was nothing but immense barracks where the spirit of the army shaped and permeated all expressions of civic and individual activity. In contrast to the Athenian democracy, no interest in arts or letters was evinced, no political life with party tensions and dissensions was allowed, the luxuries of civilized life were despised. Physical education predominated, the pedagogic effort was entirely concentrated upon building up bodies and characters hard as steel; even the teaching of ethics as far as any existed was entirely subordinated to the goal of rearing a warrior race.[2]

---

[2] Spartan children were instructed in stealing, robbing, and deceiving. They were severely punished when caught, not because they were stealing, but because they were stealing badly. In the drabness

Disobedience of even the most arbitrary commands was regarded as the greatest offense. Trade, commerce, and the arts of peace were haughtily scorned, justice and moderation derided as sentimentalism. From the cradle to the grave, men and women were regarded solely as means for strengthening the military machine.

This first example of the totalitarian state disappeared under the influence of Stoic humanism, of Christianity, and later of that rational ethicism which Grotius developed from Stoic and Christian sources. Only the Prussia of Frederick William I revived consciously the Spartan ideal as a model for the state and a conduct of life for the citizen. "Concern for arts or for science appeared to him in no way better than

---

of their life "the only relief found by the Spartans was spying on each other" (Leo Strauss in *Social Research*, November 1939, p. 517). There are many passages in ancient literature characterizing the Spartans in a way to remind one very strongly of their modern admirers. "We must indeed acknowledge that with respect to themselves and the institutions of their own country the Lacedaemonians practise virtue in a very high degree, but with respect to their conduct towards the rest of mankind, . . . one may declare that of all men with whom we are acquainted they, most conspicuously, consider what is agreeable to be honorable, and what is expedient, just" (Thucydides, Book V, 105; Loeb Classical Library, tr. by Charles Forster Smith, iii, 169). "The Lacedaemonians, who make it their first principle of action to serve their country's interest, know not anything to be just or unjust by any measure but that" (Plutarch's Lives: Agesilaus; Modern Library Edition, p. 737). The dispute between totalitarian lust for power and rational reasonableness, between "guns and butter," is well anticipated in the famous conversation between Pyrrhus and Cineas (see Plutarch's Lives: Pyrrhus; Modern Library Edition, p. 476 f.). But the reasonableness and common sense of Cineas did not prevail. Pyrrhus was inaccessible to any economic or rational motivation, he was "unable to abandon the hopes of what he so much desired."

one of the seven deadly sins. According to him, the whole race should concentrate all its energy on one thing alone, the men upon war and the women upon the household." [3] As is well known, Frederick II stated that under Frederick I Berlin had been the Athens of the north — an opinion greatly overstating the case — and that under Frederick William I it became Sparta — an opinion this time much nearer the fact. And Johann Wilhelm Gleim started his *Preussische Kriegslieder in den Feldzügen 1756 und 1757 von einem Grenadier* with the exclamation: "Berlin be Sparta!"

But although Prussia foreshadowed the totalitarian philosophy of war, its application was limited by the acceptance of the moral standards of Christianity and of common western civilization. Bismarck's statesmanship employed war as a means for definite ends. Cynically and brutally he was ready to use this means, but it was never allowed to become dominant; it was always limited to its subservient function, and at a given moment stability and security were preferred to risk and expansion. The totalitarian philosophy of war derides stability and security with its accompanying preference for a quiet and comfortable life. War becomes the highest and normative state of life; what is called peace is only a pause be-

---

[3] Carl Biedermann, *Deutschland im achtzehnten Jahrhundert*, vol. II, Part I (Leipzig, J. J. Weber, 1858), p. 167 f. Frederick William I would have abolished the Prussian Academy founded by his father if the Academy had not proposed to help in training surgeons for the army by the study of anatomy.

tween the "real" manifestations of life, preparing for them, subservient to them.

This totalitarian philosophy of war grew up under the influence of two intellectual movements, the roots of which we can trace back to the second half of the nineteenth century.[4] One of them is the belief that the substance of life and history is struggle and conflict. The application of Darwinism to the social sciences made war and strife appear as the normal manifestations of all nature, of which man was only part. Soon the accepted moral values were revealed as ill-suited to this new conception. The fundamental basis of Chancellor Hitler's *Mein Kampf* is an interpretation of man according to which he is purely a natural being, biologically determined, and inescapably subject to the "iron logic of nature," which he has to obey as animals do if he wishes to preserve or increase his strength and to be true to his "nature." In such a world strength and success alone count: the "idle dreams" of universal truth and justice disappear in the dust heap of bookishness before the triumphant march of full-blooded man. In the face of this nihilism, this twilight of all moral values, Life is exalted as the only and inexorable arbiter of all action and conduct. "World history is the world tribunal: it has always justified the stronger, the fuller, the more self-assured life, has given it the right to existence,

[4] I have tried to trace the genesis of totalitarian "Weltanschauung" in my two recent books, *Force or Reason* (Harvard University Press, 1938) and especially *Revolutions and Dictatorships* (Harvard University Press, 1939).

whether or not it was regarded as good. It has always sacrificed truth and justice to might and vitality, and doomed those peoples to death who considered truth more important than deeds, and justice more essential than might." [5]

The other movement of ideas, closely connected with the first, is the denial of universal values and truth, their relativization and "nationalization." Thus two enemies facing each other are not united any

[5] Oswald Spengler, *Der Untergang des Abendlandes*, vol. ii (Munich, C. H. Beck, 1922), p. 635. See also on p. 542: "Die Mächte des Blutes, die urwüchsigen Triebe alles Lebens, die ungebrochene körperliche Kraft treten in ihrer alten Herrschaft wieder an. Die Rasse bricht rein und unwiderstehlich hervor: der Erfolg der Stärksten und der Rest als Beute. Sie ergreift das Weltregiment, und das Reich der Bücher und Probleme erstarrt oder versinkt in Vergessenheit." ("The forces of the blood, the primitive instincts of all life, the unbroken vigor of the body resume their old domination. The rule of the race emerges pure and irresistible: the success of the strongest, and the rest as prey. It now assumes the government of the world, and the realm of books and problems becomes torpid or sinks into oblivion.") And eleven years later, in the first year of National Socialist domination, Spengler proclaimed in his *Jahre der Entscheidung*, Part i (Munich, C. H. Beck, 1933), p. 14: "Der Kampf ist die Urtatsache des Lebens, ist das Leben selbst. Der triste Zug der Weltverbesserer, der als einziges Denkmal seines Daseins Berge bedruckten Papiers auf dem Wege zurückliess, ist zu Ende" ("Struggle is the fundamental fact of life, is life itself; the weary procession of reformers, leaving as their only monument their mountains of printed paper, is now ended"). And on p. 24: "Menschliche Geschichte im Zeitalter der hohen Kulturen ist die Geschichte politischer Mächte. Die Form dieser Geschichte ist der Krieg. Auch der Friede gehört dazu. Er ist die Fortsetzung des Krieges mit anderen Mitteln. . . . Ein Staat ist das 'in Form sein' einer durch ihn gebildeten und dargestellten völkischen Einheit für wirkliche und mögliche Kriege." ("Human history in the period of highly developed civilization is the history of political powers. The form of this history is war. Peace is only part of it. It is the continuation of the war by other means. . . . A state is the 'being-in-form' of a national unit, formed and represented by it, for actual and possible wars.")

more by a moral or intellectual community above the battle fields. This lack of common moral or intellectual attitudes is always noticeable, as war in reality is a permanent phenomenon. Even in so-called peace times each nation, according to the National Socialists, has its own peculiar thought processes, develops its own science, lives according to its own standards of national ethics and honor. All bridges of understanding and communication are destroyed. Nationalism reaches here its extreme manifestation: sovereignty is not only political, it is economic and cultural as well. Not only does all hope of world cooperation become futile: the republic of letters, the oneness of mankind and civilization, no longer exist or are "unmasked" as idle cerebral fancies. Under these circumstances the word "enemy" gains a new meaning. Everybody is a potential enemy, and every enemy becomes a total enemy. The whole existence is always overshadowed by war. The army becomes the model of life, and its collectivism, as in Sparta, spreads to all fields of human endeavor, and is mistaken for socialism. This new "socialism," which is nothing but the collectivism of an army, is again proof of the strangely ambiguous use of words in our times. It was first Oswald Spengler in his *Preussentum und Sozialismus*, which he published immediately after the World War, who identified Prussianism and socialism. This socialism is, according to Spengler, "will to power, struggle for the well-being, not of the individual, but of the whole." This whole, however, is never humanity; it is a fictitious whole, called organic, of a part of mankind — a state, nation, or race — which acts as if it were the whole. Spengler carries even his prussification of socialism to the paradox of calling Frederick William I, and not Marx, the "first conscious socialist." [6]

A similar conception of "socialism" was propagated at about the same time by Moeller Van Den Bruck. For him Prussia meant a nationalistic communism or collectivism on a hierarchical and aristocratic basis. In his *Das Dritte Reich*, in which he demands the complete separation of Germany from the West (for "am Liberalismus gehen die Völker zu Grunde"), and the fulfillment of a German mission by a new Germany of which the frontiers will be those of her mission, he states that each people has its own socialism. Socialism is for him definitely opposed to any international community. German socialism means "Verwurzelung, Staffelung, Gliederung." "Where Marxism ends, there begins socialism: a German socialism, whose mission it is to supplant in the intellectual history of mankind all liberalism. This German socialism is not the task of a Third Reich. It is rather

---

[6] *Politische Schriften* (Munich, C. H. Beck), p. 43. *Ibidem*, p. vii: "Socialism, as I understand it, presupposes private enterprise with its old Germanic delight in power and plunder." About Prussia he says on p. 63: "In Preussen war ein wirklicher Staat vorhanden. Hier gab es streng genommen keinen Privatmann. Jeder, der innerhalb des mit der Exaktheit einer guten Maschine arbeitenden Systems lebte, gehörte irgendwie als Glied an." ("A real state existed in Prussia. Here, in the strict sense of the word, private individuals did not exist. Everybody who lived within the system, which worked with the precision of a good machine, was in some way part of the machine.")

its foundation."[7] This new militaristic collectivism differs, however, in one fundamental respect from its Spartan model, in its emphasis upon productive work and upon the importance of the industrial worker. The achievements of modern industrial society, with its stress upon mechanization, standardization, and disciplined team work, are not only fully accepted by the totalitarian regimes (in spite of some romantic impulses to toy with soil and primitive agrarianism), but regimented into a system of a military super-industrialism. The worker becomes a soldier, the border lines between industrial society and army become more and more fluid until they disappear, the factories become barracks, and the same discipline and devotion are demanded in both. Work becomes an obligation towards the state. The state fixes the compensations and conditions of labor, the freedom of exchange or contract is abolished, and property becomes a *fidei-commissum*. Ernst Jünger created in his *Der Arbeiter: Herrschaft und Gestalt* the apotheosis of a thoroughly mechanized and militarized worker, a modern machine-man, a member in a group closely knit together in hierarchical order and pervaded by one spirit, united for higher efficiency and external action.[8] In a similar way Mussolini stressed

[7] *Das Dritte Reich*, 3rd ed. (Hamburg, Hanseatische Verlagsanstalt, 1931), p. 67 f.

[8] Ernst Jünger, *Der Arbeiter* (Hamburg, Hanseatische Verlagsanstalt, 1932). In a former book, *Das abenteuerliche Herz* (Berlin, Frundsberg Verlag, 1929), Jünger had expressed the underlying nihilism of the Fascist attitude, its despair of any values in life, its glorification of vitality in itself: "To what purpose one exists, that

the unity of soldiers and workers, he called his *Popolo d'Italia* the "newspaper of combatants and producers." His coöperative state is the expression of an "Italian socialism," based upon presuppositions hardly different from those of "German socialism."

This worker and soldier is being trained in the totalitarian states to accept hardness of life and risk as the normal life, tragic heroism as human destiny, and to reject contemptuously any desire for a sheltered and a comfortable life, for the amenities of the ridiculed bourgeois or western civilization. In intentionally terse and striking sentences Mussolini has tried to formulate this new way of life: "Tutta la nazione deve essere militarizzata . . . Nella vita la felicità non esiste . . . Io considero la Nazione Italiana in stato permanente di guerra . . . Vivere per me è la lotta, il rischio, la tenacia . . . Il Fascista disdegna la vita comoda . . . Il credo del Fascismo è l'eroismo." [9] Whereas it is characteristic that Lenin

---

may never be learned; all so-called goals can only be pretexts of destiny. But that one exists, that is the essential. . . . For that reason this time demands one virtue above all others: that of resolution. It is essential, to find will and faith, quite apart from and irrespective of any contents of this will and faith. . . . All the fight today about flags and symbols, laws and dogmas, order and systems, is humbug. Your very horror of these quarrels reveals that you are not in need of answers, but of sharp questions, not of flags but of combats, not of order but of rebellion, not of systems but of men."

[9] "The whole nation must be militarized. . . . Happiness does not exist in life. . . . I consider the Italian nation in a permanent state of war. . . . Life for me is struggle, risk, tenacity. . . . The Fascist disdains the comfortable life. . . . The creed of Fascism is heroism." *Op. cit.*, vol. I, p. 283; II, 230; V, 238 f.; VIII, 69; IX, 43. These are only a very few examples taken at random.

and Stalin had no need to boast of their humble origin, and certainly never emphasized that they had been common soldiers in the war or had wished to do their duty and regarded their soldierly duty and experiences as the zenith of their lives, Hitler and Mussolini both stress their humble origins and above all their experiences as common soldiers in the World War.[10] Asked by Emil Ludwig of what Mussolini is proudest in his career, the head of the Italian government answered without hesitation, "Of having been a good soldier." The answer was probably sincere; it would have sounded improbable in the mouth of Bismarck or Crispi, of Lloyd George or Clemenceau, of Bethmann-Hollweg or Neville Chamberlain.

In this new philosophy of life strategic considerations of soldiery take precedence over economic well-being. Walther Rathenau, the famous German industrialist and statesman, had pronounced economics to determine our fate. "Wirtschaft ist Schicksal." In this attitude the two great currents of the later nineteenth century, liberal capitalism and socialism, had agreed. Now they are confronted with the proclamation of the precedence of politics over economics. "Politik ist Schicksal," affirms Carl Schmitt. Politics

[10] On Hitler see *Revolutions and Dictatorships*, p. 181 and 343. From Mussolini: "I am proud to be a son of laborers. I am proud to have worked with my own hands." And again: "Considero il momento più bello della mia vita quello in cui fui lacerato dalle ferite" ("I regard as the most beautiful moment of my life that in which I was wounded"). And again: "I am and I remain on the ramparts (sulla breccia); I am bound, not to my caprice, but to my soldier's post." *Op. cit.*, III, 49; IV, 18, 248.

is life and life is politics, as Oswald Spengler says; but with the discarding of economic man, the meaning of political man has been changed as fundamentally. Now arises a concept of politics which receives its meaning, not from what has been considered the normal life of society, but from the border-line case. The normal does not try any more to dominate and limit the anormal; it is the anormal, the exceptional, the *ultima ratio*, which determines and directs the normal. A German political scientist has best expressed this new attitude: "One can say that here, as elsewhere, precisely the exceptional case has a particularly decisive meaning and reveals the heart of the matter. . . . It is from this most extreme possibility that the life of men gains its specific political tension." [11] In his theory about the origins and legitimacy of right, a theory which he calls decisionism, Carl Schmitt lets right be determined by the legislator who has the power to realize and enforce the decision. Ideal justice and positive law are discarded as norms of law-making. Starting from the extraordinary situation, the *Staatsnotstand* ("Not kennt kein Gebot"), where the necessities of existence seem to demand the disregard of abstract justice or of the existing positive law, Schmitt applies this "anormal" case to the "normal" course of existence. "Right" is thus always dependent upon the concrete situation and has its source in the decision with which the supreme power-authority

[11] Carl Schmitt, *Der Begriff des Politischen* (Hamburg, Hanseatische Verlagsanstalt, 1933), p. 18.

meets the situation. "Jegliches Recht ist Situations-
recht." ("Each law corresponds to a concrete situation.") As each situation is unique and concrete,
there cannot be any general and abstract norm. Each
decision is valid only for its own situation. "Justice"
becomes the function of the power which makes the
essentially political decision; political and judicial
functions are no longer separated, although political
decisions continue to be made to appear as judicial
ones. But in practice, and frequently in theory, the
judicial function is subordinated to the political. In
his address to the Deutsche Juristentag in 1936 Rudolf
Hess repeated Treitschke's words: "Alle Rechts-
pflege ist eine politische Tätigkeit." ("All justice is
political.")

This exaltation of life over law — in Spengler's
terminology of *Dasein* over *Wachsein* — results in a
precarious existence on the rim of an abyss. Carl
Schmitt bases his concept of politics on the inescapable antagonism between friend and enemy, an antagonism as fundamental as that between good and
bad, or between the beautiful and the ugly. Political
conflicts are therefore for Schmitt not rationally or
ethically determined or solvable; they are "existential" conflicts,[12] in which existence itself is at stake.

[12] "Existential" is one of the new expressions corresponding to attitudes in Germany produced by the post-war nihilism. The "existential" political theory of Schmitt corresponds to the existential philosophy of Heidegger. In his *Der Begriff des Politischen*, p. 8, Carl Schmitt
says: "Der Feind ist in einem besonders intensiven Sinne existenziell
ein Anderer und Fremder, mit dem im extremen Fall existenzielle
Konflikte möglich sind. Derartige Konflikte können weder durch

For this political theory war is the culmination, the zenith, of political life, and hence of life in general; the inescapable friend-enemy relation dominates all life. This political philosophy corresponds to the supposed primitive combative instinct of man, who tends to regard anyone who stands in the way of the realization of his desires as a foe who has to be done away with. This concept clearly marks all the policies, internal and foreign, of Chancellor Hitler's government. Civilized statesmanship, on the other hand, consists in finding the ways and means to overcome the primitive instincts by compromise, by patient negotiations, by an effort at reciprocity, and above all by the acknowledgment of universally binding law.[13]

Thus from all sides war is acclaimed as the supreme moment of life. Whereas in the western nations after the World War the war itself was recognized as a great calamity and tragedy, a very

eine im voraus getroffene generelle Normierung, noch durch den Spruch eines 'unbeteiligten' und deshalb 'unparteiischen' Dritten entschieden werden." ("The enemy is in a most intensive sense existentially another and an alien, with whom in the extreme case conflicts are possible in which existence itself is at stake. Such conflicts can not be decided by a general agreement previously concluded, nor by the judgment of a third party which is not involved and therefore impartial.") And on p. 15: "Der Krieg folgt aus der Feindschaft, denn diese ist seinsmässige Negierung eines anderen Seins." ("War is the result of enmity, for enmity is the existential negation of the existence of another.")

[13] See my *Force or Reason*, p. 19 f. Schmitt says *op. cit.*, p. 48: "Die Höhepunkte der grossen Politik sind zugleich die Augenblicke, in denen der Feind in konkreter Deutlichkeit als Feind erblickt wird." ("The culminating points of great politics are the moments in which the enemy is visualised in concrete clarity as the enemy.")

large part of the German people did not regard the war as a tragedy or calamity, but the defeat. They blamed all the ills, which the western nations blamed on the war, on the peace treaties. Whereas the western nations blamed themselves for having got into the war and having made the peace, the large majority of the Germans never blamed themselves, but blamed only the enemy for having devised the peace. National Socialist propaganda increased this growing estrangement from the west by glorifying the war and the German army, and by strengthening the already-too-strong German tendencies to see the source of all their maladjustments, not in their own faults or shortcomings, but in the machinations of their "enemies." "We National Socialists know that the Great War from 1914 to 1918 will live in the memory of later generations as a mythical great deed without equal." [14] Hitler's racial theory had the effect of destroying the remaining sense of reciprocity and responsibility in the German people and of convincing them that on account of their superior qualities they are always right and that the heroic warrior ideal which they have cultivated justified their world domination. "The struggle for a German rebirth is a struggle for the assertion of the German hero ideal against the democratic shop-keeper ideal," says Rosenberg, and Hitler praises Germany because she was "a most magnificent example of a nation, created on the

[14] Alfred Rosenberg, *Das Wesengefüge des National Sozialismus*, 4th ed. (Munich, Eher, 1933), p. 9.

foundations of pure power-politics. Prussia, the germ
cell of the Reich, arose through radiant heroism
('durch strahlendes Heldentum') and not through
financial manœuvres or commercial transactions; and
the Reich itself was only the most glorious reward for
power-political leadership and warrior's courage in
face of death." [15]

Thus the pacifism which became predominant in
the western democracies after the World War was
stamped out by the new philosophy in Fascist countries. "War is to the man what maternity is to the
woman. I do not believe in perpetual peace; not only
do I not believe in it, but I find it depressing and a
negation of all the fundamental virtues of man." [16]
The preamble to the statute of the Italian Fascist party
of December 20, 1929, prides itself that "from its beginnings until now, the Party has always thought of
itself as in a state of war. Fascism is above all a faith

[15] Alfred Rosenberg, Der Mythus des 20. Jahrhunderts, 37th ed.
(Munich, Hoheneichen Verlag, 1934), p. 639. Adolf Hitler, Mein
Kampf (Munich, Eher, 1933), vol. i, p. 169.
[16] Mussolini, op. cit., vol. ix, p. 98. Well known are the anti-pacifist
passages in the often translated article by Mussolini on the doctrine
of Fascism in the Enciclopedia Italiana. Translations can be found in
Alfred Zimmern, Modern Political Doctrines (London, Oxford University Press, 1939), p. 31 ff., and in Michael Oakeshott, The Social
and Political Doctrines of Contemporary Europe (Cambridge University Press, 1939), p. 164 ff. See there too on p. 180 f. the two Fascist
Decalogues. The most characteristic passages are: "Above all, Fascism
believes neither in the possibility nor in the utility of perpetual peace.
. . .War alone brings up to their highest tension all human energies
and puts the stamp of nobility upon the peoples who have the courage
to meet it. . . . Fascism carries over this anti-pacifist spirit even into
the lives of individuals. It is education for combat. . . . The Fascist
looks on life as duty, ascent, conquest."

under the impulse of which the Italians work as soldiers, pledged to achieve victory in the struggle between the nation and its enemies." This attitude had already been foreseen by Mussolini during the years of the World War, and by Oswald Spengler in his *Decline of the West*, where he characterized the new time in the following words: "Life is harsh. It leaves only one choice, that between victory and defeat, not between war and peace. . . . Pacifism implies the personal renunciation of war on the part of the great majority, but with that also the unadmitted readiness to become the prey of others who make no such renunciation. It begins with the desire for general reconciliation, and it ends with no one stirring a hand as long as the misfortune befalls only the neighbor." [17]

For outside consumption and for purposes of diplomatic war, the spokesmen and advocates of the new philosophy of totalitarian war may speak sometimes of their desire for peace and may indulge themselves in some kind of pacifist propaganda, strictly forbidden under heaviest penalties to their own subjects. But even a cursory perusal of the fundamental sources of the new philosophy, whether in the writings and speeches of Mussolini or Hitler, or in the vast literary output of their enthusiastic followers, reveals the un-

[17] *Op. cit.*, p. 538, 545 f. See also in his *Politische Schriften*, p. 55: "War is always the higher form of human existence, and states exist for the sake of war. . . . Even were a weary and lifeless humanity desirous of renouncing wars, it would become instead of the subject of war, the object for whom and with whom others would wage wars."

bridgeable gulf between their own profession of faith and their pragmatic toying with the pleasantness of peace. On August 25, 1934, Mussolini declared: "We are becoming and we shall become ever more, because we will it, a military nation. Because we are not afraid of words, I shall add: a militarist one. To say it fully: a warrior nation (*guerriera*), which will be endowed to an ever higher degree with the virtue of obedience, of sacrifice, of dedication to the fatherland. That means that the whole life of the nation, the political as well as the economic and spiritual life, must be directed towards our military necessities. . . . I recall to you that the military forces represent the essential element of the hierarchy among the nations. Nothing has yet been found which can substitute for that which is the clearest, most tangible and most determining expression of the complex force of a whole people: that is, the size, the prestige, the power of its arms — on land, on sea, and in the air." [18]

Dr. Robert Ley, one of the leading spokesmen of present-day Germany, expressed himself with the same forceful lucidity in an editorial in the newspaper *Angriff* on March 27, 1940. He said:

"War is not in contrast to peace but simply another form of expression of the uninterrupted battle of nations and men. It is an expression of the highest and best in manhood. In spite of the difficulties it brings and the sacrifices it demands, we thank Provi-

[18] *Op. cit.*, vol. IX, p. 113–115. See also p. 197 f.; vol. III, p. 60; vol. IV, p. 294; vol. V, p. 29, 118, 181; and passim.

dence that it constantly calls forth our men to their last and greatest effort.

"In this war lies the rebirth of our nation. Every war demands a blood sacrifice from the men of the nation. They should give their blood gladly for thus they equalize that which every mother gives at the birth of a child.

"In nations living in 'eternal peace' manhood dries up and all the virtues that make man lovable to woman degenerate.

"One cannot demand of mothers that they uninterruptedly give the nation children without man bringing his blood sacrifice. Therefore war is not the wrath of God but a blessing of God."

In the totalitarian regimes society is entirely subordinated to the state and even destroyed by it. There is no individual or social sphere outside the state. But even the state is not a true state; it is not more than the apparatus of one party which entirely identifies itself with the state and society, absorbing all their functions. The great difference even between Bismarcko-Wilhelmian Germany and the state created by National Socialism was clearly indicated by the declarations of the respective leaders at the outbreak of the great wars. In 1914 Emperor William II declared that he no longer recognized any parties among the Germans and that he stretched out his hands to all his internal opponents for coöperation and internal peace. At the outbreak of the war in 1939 Chancellor Hitler did not invite the coöperation of any internal opponents, but on the contrary threatened them in terms unusually violent, even for him. The famous Protestant theologian, Karl Barth, rightly pointed out that the National Socialist state consists in the disintegration of the just or right state, that it is a state only in so far as it is not yet National Socialist in certain remnants carried over from the old state, but that otherwise it is an anarchy tempered by tyranny, or a tyranny tempered by anarchy.[19] The disappearing social order is replaced by an extension and imitation of the order of the army. The terminology of war, warriors, and struggle is applied to every phase of life, even the most civilian. All differences between the military and other walks of life are gradually abolished until the totality of life is subordinated to the set of values of the army, and farmers and teachers, industrialists and scholars are turned into soldiers of the regime.[20] As in an army, discipline

[19] *Die Kirche und die politische Frage von Heute* (Zollikon, Evangelische Buchhandlung, 1939), p. 35. This remarkable book has been published in an English translation, *The Church and the Political Question of Our Day* (New York, Scribner, 1939).

[20] The editor of the *Historische Zeitschrift*, Professor Karl Alexander von Müller, ends an editorial postscript about the war in the issue published September 15, 1939 (160, 3, p. 680): "It is in this battle of souls that we find the section of the trenches which is also entrusted to the German science of history. It will mount on guard. The watch word has been given by Hegel: The spirit of the universe gave the command to advance; such command will find itself blindly obeyed."

At the same time the lack of that chivalry which is so characteristic of non-totalitarian or real armies is astonishing in the totalitarian regimes. This lack expresses itself in the ostentatious feeling of superiority against weaker armies, in the undignified persecution of and brutality against defenseless groups, in the scorn heaped upon de-

and hierarchy, appeal to comradeship, and readiness to sacrifice are stressed. The personality of the leader gets full scope and is elevated by the amorphism of the masses beneath it. The fate of the individual in a nation which has become an army has been ably formulated in Mussolini's famous words: "In the Fascist state the individual is not suppressed, but rather multiplied, just as in a regiment a soldier is not weakened, but multiplied, by the number of his comrades." The National Socialist youth exalted as its educational and social ideal the *Männerbund*, a military order after the model of the Teutonic Knights or the Prussian officers' corps. "The principle," wrote Hitler, "which in its time made the Prussian army the most wonderful instrument of the German people, must in the future become the principle of the structure of our whole conception of the state: authority of every leader downwards and responsibility upwards." [21] The totalitarian philosophy of war has been aptly summed up by Carl Schmitt: "War is the essence of everything. The nature of the total war determines the nature and form of the totalitarian state." [22]

feated foes, in the complete absence of any sense or feeling of reciprocity.

[21] *Mein Kampf*, p. 501. See also p. 734.

[22] "Totaler Feind, Totaler Krieg, Totaler Staat" in *Völkerbund und Völkerrecht*, Jg. 4, p. 139 ff. (June 1937). "Im Kriege steckt der Kern der Dinge. Von der Art des totalen Krieges her, bestimmen sich Art und Gestalt der Totalität des Staates." ("War is the essence of everything. The form of total war determines the form of the total state.") On the efforts of National Socialist science to arrive at a theory of international law, see the excellent book by Eduard Bristler, *Die Völker-*

This philosophy of war gains even greater importance by the fact that in a war in which a totalitarian nation is involved we do not find one nation fighting against another as equal participants in a common humanity. The totalitarian nation fights inspired by its consciousness of a unique mission, the *Sendungsbewusstsein*, which is fulfilled in the war and invests its fight and victory with an almost sacral character. The racial theory, as evolved by the National Socialists, amounts to a new naturalistic religion for which the German people are the *corpus mysticum* and the army the priesthood. The new faith of biological determinism, fundamentally opposed to all transcendent and to all humanist religion, bestows upon the people an immense strength in their permanent total war against every other conception of man, whether Christian or rational. The people now represent the *Reich*, the realm of salvation; the enemy represents the *Gegenreich*; it becomes as much of a mystical and mythical fiction as the *Reich* itself; only that the one is invested with all imaginable virtues, and the other with all imaginable, and sometimes even unimaginable, vices. One of the weaknesses of this position consists in the fact that, whereas the *Reich* is a constant factor, the *Gegenreich* is a variable factor, according to circumstances, the political exigencies of one moment putting up another adversary than

rechtslehre des Nationalsozialismus (Zürich, Europa Verlag, 1938), and more generally Edmond Vermeil, *Doctrinaires de la Révolution Allemande* (Paris, Fernand Sorlot, 1938).

those of another moment. Here Chancellor Hitler made a master-move by pointing out the Jews as the *Gegenreich*,[23] and by identifying all his enemies with Judaism. Thus he could "unmask" the accidental enemy of the hour, Russia and Communism, Great Britain and Democracy, France and the United States, President Roosevelt and capitalism, in short, whoever seemed to stand in a concrete situation in the way of the fulfillment of Germany's wishes, as an instrument of the devil, opposing the march towards salvation of the *Reich*. This attitude gives to the totalitarian politics at the same time an immense flexibility and, to its own followers, the appearance of a great persistency. Spengler had foreseen this attitude when he defined the new imperialist Cæsarism which he saw coming as "that type of government which, in spite of all constitutional and philosophical formulation, is by its inherent nature lacking utterly in defined form." [24]

[23] *Mein Kampf*, p. 355. "Among our people the personification of the devil, as the symbol of everything evil, takes on the actual appearance and figure of the Jew." On the mystical character of the race see Alfred Rosenberg, *Der Mythus des 20. Jahrhunderts*, p. 114: "Heute erwacht aber ein neuer Glaube: der Mythus des Blutes, der Glaube, mit dem Blute auch das göttliche Wesen des Menschen überhaupt zu verteidigen. Der mit hellstem Wissen verkörperte Glaube, dass das nordische Blut jenes Mysterium darstellt, welches die alten Sakramente ersetzt und überwunden hat." ("Today a new faith awakens: the myth of the blood, the faith that by defending his blood we defend also the divine nature of man. The faith, embodied in scientific clarity, that the Nordic blood represents that mystery which has replaced and conquered the ancient sacraments.") See also pp. 119 and 529.

[24] *Der Untergang des Abendlandes*, vol. II, p. 541. In reality the Gegenreich for National Socialism and Fascism is everything universal, everything that believes in the oneness of mankind, in common human aspirations, in a final harmony: Christianity in all its forms,

This flexibility allows the substitution of one enemy for another most abruptly and enables the leader to direct the almost mystical totalitarian hatred of his followers against the most diverse objects. That explains the startling change in the attitude of the leader of the anti-Comintern pact towards communism and the Soviet Union after August 1939. Only a very short while ago the "destruction of Bolshevism was regarded as a fundamental right of the law of the nations and to this extent an elementary duty." It was proclaimed that "the Soviet Union must be expelled from the juridical community of nations" and that the League of Nations was "no community based on law any more, because it had recognized the total enemy of right and law as *de jure* equal." [25]

liberalism, humanism, rationalism, capitalism, communism, freemasonry, the ideas of 1789, democracy, etc., even down to the Rotarian International or any of the most innocuous forms of human coöperation or civilized intercourse.

[25] E. H. Bockhoff, *Völker-Recht gegen Bolschewismus* (Berlin, Institut zur wissenschaftlichen Erforschung der Soviet Union, 1937), pp. 238, 228, 99. This book had the honor of an introduction by the Reichsminister of Justice, Dr. Frank, who welcomed it as a contribution to the "struggle for the immortality and strength of the idea of right generally." In an article "Das Lebensrecht des deutschen Volkes" (*Deutsche Juristenzeitung*, 1936, p. 342) Karl Lohmann said: "As France allowed herself to conclude a pact of guarantee even with the devil himself (the author meant the Franco-Soviet pact), she created such a situation of menace that the measure of injustice necessarily came to overflow."

Mussolini also changed his attitude, this time with regard to Prussian militarism. On April 8, 1918, he said: "No man of good will, even not the last befuddled brain, could any longer believe that it is not Germany which did wish the war, and that it is not Germany which wishes to continue the war in order to reduce the whole world into a horrible Prussian barracks." *Op. cit.*, vol. 1, p. 306. Six years later he proclaimed as the aim of Fascism "non la caserma Prussiana, ma la

The totalitarian army gains its strength not only from the concentration of the whole national and all individual life upon war. It draws its main inspiration from the totalitarian vision according to which each individual war is nothing but a step towards imposing the new way of life upon the whole of mankind. The totalitarian army knows itself as the instrument of a national will, aspiring to the highest goal: to make the nation not only a powerful nation in the Bismarckian sense, but a world nation for which its world-day has arrived with the adoption of the new philosophy which is destined to become the new faith of mankind. Spengler defines as the duty of the German youth "to work out a new mode of political will and action from the newly formed conditions of the twentieth century, to bring to light new forms, methods, and ideas, which like the ideas of the French Revolution and the customs of the English House of Commons will spread as models from one land to the other, until the history of the coming time progresses in forms whose beginnings will in the future be found in Germany." [26] The German master-race feels the

---

nostra caserma." *Op. cit.*, vol. IV, p. 321. Fourteen years later he introduced the Prussian goose-step into the Italian army and entirely Prussianized Italian life.

[26] *Politische Schriften*, p. 146. Spengler foresaw two revolutions, the revolution of the lower classes and the revolution of the colored races, class war and racial war. He regarded Prussian Germany as the savior of the "white" world against these two revolutions. But he did not foresee that National Socialist Germany which vulgarized and materialized his teaching, as they did with that of his master Nietzsche, would become itself the center of race war and would ally herself against western civilization at one time with Japan, at another time

mission of bringing the new world order. The same vision enlivens the grandiose picture which Mussolini unfolds before the eyes of Italian youth. In 1932 he proclaimed proudly: "From now on the appeal to the forces of youth resounds: the Nation which has taken the lead, which has anticipated by a decade the action of other countries, is Italy"; and two years later, reviewing the astonishing developments of the preceding luster, he boasted: "Since 1929 Fascism has become not merely an Italian phenomenon but a world phenomenon." The essence of Fascism he defines as Spengler and the National Socialists do: an absolute revolution against western civilization, against Anglo-Saxon liberalism and against the achievements and consequences of the French Revolution. "We represent a new principle in the world, we represent the clear-cut, categorical, definitive antithesis of the whole democratic world . . . , of the whole world, to say it in one word, of the immortal principles of 1789." From this starting point, he assured the people of Milan in a speech on October 25, 1932, of the coming world leadership of Fascist Italy. "Today, with a fully tranquil conscience I say to you, immense multitude, that the twentieth century will be the century of Fascism, the century

---

with Soviet Russia, the representative of class war. Spengler regarded it as the hour of greatest danger for western civilization should race war and class war combine. "This possibility lies in the nature of things, and neither of the two revolutions will scorn the help of the other only because it is contemptuous of the other's bearer. Common hatred extinguishes mutual contempt." (*Ibid.*, p. 164.)

of Italian power, the century during which Italy will become for the third time the leader of mankind (*la direttrice della civiltà humana*), because outside of our principles there is no salvation, neither for the individuals, nor even less for the peoples." [27]

The totalitarian philosophy of war makes wars at present fought by the totalitarian states fundamentally different from the wars of the nineteenth century and even from the first World War. It is for this reason that all analogies drawn from the first World War remain superficial and do not touch the real problems involved in the war which started in 1939. As the Fascist imperialism of the thirties of our century is fundamentally different in its methods and aims from the liberal imperialism at the turn of the century — in spite of certain similarities and in spite of the confusing use of the same word for both — so the word "war" has acquired an entirely different meaning in the totalitarian states. For the liberal state, war is a hateful necessity at some given moment, something abnormal and even monstrous. Recog-

---

[27] *Op. cit.*, vol. VIII, p. 232; vol. IX, p. 32; vol. V, p. 311; vol. VIII, p. 131. The world leadership of Fascist Rome resounds in many other messages of Mussolini: "In questo mondo oscuro, tormentato e già vacillante, la salvezza non puo venire che della verità di Roma e da Roma verrà" ("In this obscure, tormented, and already vacillating world, salvation can come only from the truth of Rome, and from Rome it will come"); and "La Rivoluzione fascista non è soltanto il privilegio e lo sforzo dell'Italia, ma la parola d'ordine e la speranza del mondo" ("The Fascist revolution is not only the privilege and strength of Italy, but the word of order and the hope of the world"). These last two quotations are from vol. VIII, pp. 140 and 254. On National Socialism in this respect see: *Revolutions and Dictatorships*, pp. 352 ff., 370 f.

nizing the interdependence and common interests of all men and the equality of all peoples, liberal statesmen strive for the creation of an international order which will eliminate war altogether. Wars exist, in the liberal conception, only as a result of the shortcomings of the political and social order which in a not-too-distant future may be overcome by the rational efforts of man. In the totalitarian philosophy war is the normal and welcome concomitant of all life, the supreme manifestation of vitality and virtue, an unalterable and dominating part of the whole system. Ultimately these two different and even opposite concepts of war rest upon two different concepts of the nature and destiny of man.

ACADEMIC FREEDOM IN OUR TIME

Il fascismo vuol rifare non le forme della vita umana, ma il contenuto, l'uomo, il carattere, la fede. E a questo fine vuole disciplina, e autorità che scenda addentro negli spiriti, e vi domini incontrastata.

Fascismo: Dottrina: Idee fondamentali.
ENCICLOPEDIA ITALIANA, vol. XIV, p. 848

[Fascism wants to remake, not the forms of human life, but its content: man, character, faith. And to this end it wants discipline, and authority that enters into the spirits [of men] and there governs unopposed.]

Academic Freedom in Our Time

ACADEMIC freedom in the present meaning of the phrase is a product of recent times. Originally academic freedom meant the administrative and judicial autonomy of the university corporation of teachers and students. It was one of the many "freedoms" upon which medieval life was based. It did not and could not imply *Lehrfreiheit*, a notion entirely alien to the Middle Ages and to early modern times. Academic freedom in the modern sense is a product of the epoch of the Enlightenment, of liberalism and rationalism, of the triumph of intellectual and moral individualism. Therefore we find academic freedom today, with the great Central European counter-revolution against enlightenment, liberalism, and individualism, again being threatened in its existence.

Academic freedom is, above all, a duty of the teacher. It is, to use a word from Cicero, his duty never to say anything false and never to dare to withhold anything true. "Nam quis nescit primam esse historiae legem, ne quid falsi dicere audeat? Deinde ne quid veri non audeat?" [1] The teacher is expected to present to his students the whole truth, as he understands it in the light of his research and thought. He should put his whole individuality into his teaching with no guide but his individual con-

[1] Cicero, *De Oratore*, II, 15.

science. Only in this way can he present to the student, and make the student share in, the dignity of spiritual and intellectual endeavor and the seriousness which it exacts. The teacher must be free to speak his mind; the student must experience his effort at truth. This is impossible in totalitarian countries where the objectivity of truth and thereby the dignity of the teaching profession are not recognized.

Different from academic freedom as a duty of the teacher is academic freedom as a right of the teacher, the right to speak the truth as he understands it. This right is no professional right of the teacher alone, it is part of the general right to freedom of every citizen, the freedom to think for himself and to express his thoughts by word and in print. The academic teacher does not possess more rights than other citizens, he has only greater duties. Everybody has the right to speak the truth. The teacher *must* speak the truth. This is the meaning of his calling.

Academic freedom is therefore conceivable only within a certain intellectual order, that of individual rights, based upon that interpretation of man's nature and his place in history which we call liberalism. This attitude is not a "natural" birthright of man. It is a product of a great historical struggle, which started in the sevententh century and was won, at least for the time being, in the nineteenth century for Western humanity. This struggle, waged by Milton and Locke, by Grotius and Condorcet, by the Encyclopaedists and Kant, produced all the liberties, which are fundamentally one liberty. Academic freedom is nothing in itself, no abstraction which can be invoked at will; it is an indissoluble part of the whole system of liberalism, of individual rights, of a rational order, and only conceivable within it.

There is much confusion today with regard to this point. Academic freedom, the right to free speech, and the right to self-determination, are today often invoked by those who do not believe in them and in their liberal foundations, and who wish to use them solely for the purpose of undermining and destroying these liberties and their foundation. Enemies of liberalism should not be allowed to claim and use the instruments of liberalism in their fight against it. It is characteristic that a recent writer on Italian Fascism could say of Mussolini's paper, *Popolo d'Italia*, that "no other newspaper in Italy took such advantage of the freedom from legal and political responsibility which the Italian press enjoyed." It used its freedom to destroy that freedom entirely.

For all these freedoms are nothing when dissociated from their common root, which alone makes them possible. They are a corollary of a certain interpretation of the nature of man and his place in history. It is faith, to use the words of Thomas Jefferson, in the "illimitable freedom of the human mind," in universal reason, shared, at least potentially, by every human being, irrespective of his class or caste, faith or creed, birth or race. The faith without which all academic freedom and all rights of the individual become meaningless is a faith in the dignity and equality of all individuals as rational beings or as created in the image of God. From this assumption alone we can arrive at the conclusion that men are able and entitled to think independently, that truth can be found by their efforts and common discussion.

This free discussion appears to us as the only way in which science and truth can be promoted. Scholarship can prosper only by an unhampered free intercourse above all the frontiers of states, creeds, races, and classes. A totalitarian order, whether based upon the absolutization of the race or of the class or of any other relative division of mankind, undermines the development of truth and of scholarship, where the contribution of every fellowman is welcome only according to its intrinsic value.[2] Liberalism presupposes the existence of a universal truth, of universally applicable laws. It accepts the objectivity of science and of the search for truth. The Communist or the Fascist will ask who you are, to which class or race you belong, before evaluating or accepting any contribution of yours in the field of scholarship. The

[2] There is an essential difference between Communism and Fascism. Communism destroys the foundations of scholarship, the possibility of human freedom and of human dignity. It restricts "man" to "proletarian." But ultimately Communism believes in the abolition of all separating and dividing exclusiveness, in one universal, rational truth, although in a future which may never dawn. After all, Communism is a grandchild of Hegel. Fascism, in all its forms, denies any future universal truth, while it strengthens, idealizes, and absolutizes the exclusive divisions of mankind with their different kinds of "truth." It thus proclaims the eternal anarchism of all values. Only its dynamism is universal in the sense that it is unlimited and illimitable. It will not and cannot rest until the whole of mankind acknowledges it.

liberal will ask what you have to say, and accept the contribution at its objective value in the universal and unceasing search for truth. Academic freedom and freedom of scholarship are only possible within the system of liberalism.

Thus academic freedom has been accepted in the Western world as part of the liberal order. Certainly there are everywhere failures to live up to it. Academic freedom, like all liberties, is never completely realized. Although we may not always live up to it, it remains before us as a regulative ideal, a demand, and a reproach. Even if liberties, in a liberal order, are denied again and again, they can be fought for, and those who in actual fact deny them, find themselves on the defensive. In theory, at least, they have to pay lip-service to them, to recognize their general applicability. The shameful situation in Russia, in Italy, in Germany, today does not consist in the fact that in some or many cases the freedom to speak one's thoughts is denied, but in that there is no battle being waged for it, that graveyard silence reigns, that the ideal as such, the objectivity of truth, is denied.

We see the results of this attitude in the press and literary productions of the totalitarian countries with their completely one-sided and distorted views, their ludicrous judgments on the forces at work in history and in the contemporary world. Of course foolish opinions can also be put forward in liberal countries, but here they can be combated and rectified, the public can make its choice. In totalitarian countries no defense exists against the dulling of the intellect, against obscurantism, against cutting loose from world currents. Today even the language used in the totalitarian countries has nothing in common with the language used outside of these countries. The same words do in no way convey the same meaning.

Academic freedom is an indispensable part of the democratic, liberal order. But this order is denied today not only for Italy or Germany, but universally. A new interpretation of man and of his place in history wishes to impose itself upon the whole of mankind. (It is not a question of certain nations, although certain nations, for historical reasons, succumb to it more easily; it is not the problem of a fight against Italy or Germany, but against the fundamental attitude which denies the equality of men, the universality of truth, the dignity of reason.) This new attitude threatens academic freedom and free scholarship as it threatens all other freedom. In such a situation the academic teacher has a greater responsibility, to be wide awake to the dangers threatening not only academic freedom but the whole liberal tradition which produced academic freedom. He has no right to withdraw into an ivory tower, to care only for academic freedom. Academic freedom lives and dies with the whole liberal order.

If we care for academic freedom we have to fight for freedom generally, in the universities and in all other walks of life, in the United States, and everywhere. The enemies of freedom by their tactics destroy one isolated position after another; they can do it because they do not encounter united opposition. The forces for freedom are divided, not only among nations but also among professions. The attack, however, is a totalitarian attack. The fight for academic freedom is today, when liberalism itself is threatened, no longer a professional fight for the factual realization of a generally acknowledged principle. It is part of a fight for the survival of the fundamental values of liberalism for everybody and everywhere. It is a special application of the most fundamental battle in which man can be enlisted, the fight centered around the interpretation of the values governing the life and history of man.

THE PROBLEM OF CENTRAL EUROPE

In this gray hour, one joy is still our lot:
To sit beside the hearth with friends, some few;
Bar out the din of Europe; turn anew
Our thoughts to happier days of old, and roam
In reverie, and meditate on home.

How should we think of those fresh seas of blood,
Those tears that cover Poland like a flood,
Or of that glory, which reverberates still?
To think of these we had no heart, no will.

For now so sorely racked our nation lies
That even Valour, with her watchful eyes,
Can only wring her hands, and see it agonize.

ADAM MICKIEWICZ, *Pan Tadeusz*, Epilogue
(Translated by Oliver Elton)

The Legacy of the Habsburgs

THE Habsburg duke Frederick the Younger, who died in 1493 as the Emperor Frederick III, was throughout his long life and rule neither a successful nor a remarkable personality. He was threatened by several revolts of his own subjects, was defeated by his external enemies, was unable to maintain the position of his family in Bohemia and Hungary, and contributed considerably to the weakening of the imperial position in Germany. German historiography rarely has had anything good to say of him. Nevertheless, this emperor of little energy, who seemed "asleep on his throne," prepared the final union of all Habsburg lands and laid the foundations of a world empire through the marriage of his son with the heiress of Burgundy. For more than three centuries after his death the imperial dignity was to remain almost uninterruptedly connected with his house, so that Empire and Habsburg became synonymous. This mediocre prince must have had a strong premonition of the coming greatness of his house. He expressed it in the strange combination of the five vowels which he used to inscribe on buildings and belongings. In his own interpretation they meant: "Alles Erdreich ist Österreich untertan" ("All the earth is subject to

Austria") or "Austriae est imperare orbi universo" ("Austria must rule the universe"). This naïve confidence was, in the stress and storm of later periods, reinterpreted into the still confident but rather obscure apocalyptic "Austria erit in orbe ultima" ("Austria will be the last on earth").

The five vowels accompanied the house of Austria through its unprecedented rise and its later decline, always singling it out from the other dynasties and countries of the earth. Austria was a unique state. It was a territorial state and at the same time a universal empire, fusing into its service the two great universal ideas of western Christianity: the succession to the Roman Empire and the guardianship of the Catholic church. It was a product of German expansion and colonization, and it was at the same time multilingual and multiracial from the beginning; it stretched from the outskirts of the ill-defined and amorphous German *Lebensraum* into the much better defined and geographically more organic *Donauraum*, of which it became the organizing and strategic center. It was turned against the east, against Turkey, and much later against Russia, and at the same time against the west, against France and Italy; but though it was turned against them in defense, it was wide open to their cultural influences, and its cultural universalism radiated as a civilizing influence in all directions. Thus the question of the meaning of this unique political, cultural, and geographic entity arose. In the nineteenth century, the age of nationalism, Austria seemed to many a relic from dynastic and universal-istic times. Or was its existence a necessity corre-sponding to some geographic and historical reality? The year 1918 posed these questions with the im-mediate urgency of a great political catastrophe. Eastern-central Europe was divided up; as one of its independent parts an Austria remained, reduced to the lands held by the early Habsburgs. Was it merely a German territory? Or had it, through history and destiny, acquired its own peculiar character, certainly as German as that of the Swiss Confederation, and, nevertheless, distinctly Austrian, rooted in its own past and with its own future beneficial to all Danu-bian peoples and to Europe? These questions formed the center of discussion of Austria's historiography after 1918.

A leading Austrian historian, Heinrich Ritter von Srbik, tried in his monumental *Deutsche Einheit, Idee und Wirklichkeit vom Heiligen Reich bis Königgrätz* to answer these questions from the Pan-German point of view.[1] To Austria, Srbik ascribed a supranational

[1] "Die österreichische Idee erschien mir stets als eine im Wesen deutsche Idee, das österreichische Werden vieler Jahrhunderte schien mir nur durch die Reichsverbundenheit ermöglicht, und Österreichs 'historische Mission' sah ich ebenso wie seine Gegenwart und Zukunft nur in der unlösbaren Verklammerung mit der Gesamtnation gegeben." ("The Austrian idea appeared to me always as an essentially German idea, the growth of Austria during the many centuries appeared to me only possible through its connection with the German Reich, and I could see Austria's historical mission as well as its present and future only in an indissoluble union with the whole German nation.") (*Deutsche Einheit*, vol. 1, p. 10). Srbik, answering his opponents in "Zur gesamtdeutschen Geschichtsauffassung," *Historische Zeitschrift*, CLVI (1937), 229–62, envisaged in 1937 the German Reich as "der feste na-

mission, the unification of the many nationalities of
central and central-eastern Europe; but this unification was to be accomplished under undisputed German
leadership, and, in the first place, for the greatness
and growth of the German nation. Here, however, the question arises whether the future of Austria
and of central Europe could be erected in the nineteenth and twentieth centuries on such a foundation.
At the end of his second volume, in discussing the
situation after Austria had lost Lombardy and with it
the hope of any vital influence in the south, Srbik
restated his credo: "Austria had to turn to its German
hegemony; its task was to strengthen again its dimin-
ished authority as German leader and to remain a
German power, as was its destiny and mission" (II,
408 f.). Was that really Austria's destiny and mission? May it not have been, as the Czech historian

---

tionalstaatliche Kern der Erdteilsmitte, mit ihm in festester nationaler
Lebensgemeinschaft verbunden das heutige rein deutsche Österreich,
ferner angegliedert auf der Grundlage der Achtung ihrer Staatlichkeit und der Achtung ungehemmten Lebensrechtes ihrer Völker die
ostmitteleuropäische Staatenwelt" ("the firm national kernel of the
center of the continent, connected with it in the strongest possible
national community the present purely German Austria, and beyond
it all the states of Eastern Central Europe, connected with Germany
on the basis of respect for their nationhood and of respect for the
unhampered right to live of their peoples"). After this adherence to
the National Socialist program for the reordering of central and central-eastern Europe, it is not astonishing that Professor Srbik welcomed
enthusiastically the annexation of Bohemia by the National Socialists
in an article in the *Völkischer Beobachter*, March 19, 1939, entitled
"Deutsche Führung – der Segen des Böhmischen Raums." He did not
inquire whether the respect for the "Staatlichkeit und ungehemmtes
Lebensrecht" of the Czech people had been preserved in that
"blessing."

František Palacký suggested,[2] the federation of the many nationalities of eastern-central Europe in an economic unit and on a footing of complete equality, to enrich them in mutual coöperation socially and culturally and to protect them against subjugation by the two great nations of central and eastern Europe, the Germans and the Russians? Geographic and economic reasons, the preservation of peace in Europe, the interests of the smaller nationalities themselves — all seemed to point in the same direction. The history of Austria from 1848 to 1867 can be written, as Ritter von Srbik has done so eloquently, from the point of view of Austria as predominantly a part of Germany and of a system of German rule over *Mittel-Europa*. It could, however, also be written as the story of a frustrated attempt at the transformation of Austria into a federation in which the German element and the capital of Vienna would have played — politically, economically, and culturally — a most important part but in which there would have been no German or Magyar predominance. In spite of Austria's exclusion from Germany in 1866, the

[2] Palacký formulated his point of view in the letter which he sent on April 11, 1848, to the German parliament at Frankfort and where he wrote the famous sentence: "Certainly if the Austrian state were not already existent, then we would have to create it as quickly as possible in the interests of Europe, nay in the interests of humanity itself." The same point of view was expanded in an article, "On Centralization and National Equality in Austria," which Palacký published on December 21, 1849, and in his longer essay *The Idea of the Austrian State*, published in the spring of 1865. The latter is a plea for federalization as against the then foreshadowed dualism which two years later shattered the hopes of Palacký.

dualism of 1867 and later the foreign policy of the dual monarchy tried to preserve a predominantly German "mission" for Austria. This attitude necessarily provoked the resistance of the non-German and non-Magyar nationalities in Austria-Hungary. Instead of becoming an important and necessary factor for the stability of central Europe, the Habsburg empire was disintegrated by the struggle of the nationalities. The peace treaties of 1919, by sanctioning its collapse and disorganizing the whole area into small and weak states, opened the way for the domination of central and central-eastern Europe by Berlin and gave Germany a chance for expansion along the Danube unhoped for even by Bismarck. Wisely, the peace treaties tried, in an otherwise unwise and unfortunate situation, to keep the German remnant of Austria independent. It was recognized that the annexation of Vienna by Berlin would become dangerous to the balance of power in Europe and to the consolidation of peace in the new and still very unstable order in the Danubian Basin. Once in possession of Vienna, Berlin could, with incomparably greater efficiency, ruthlessness, and military resources, reëstablish that which German nationalists regarded as Austria's mission — the strategic, political, and economic German hegemony over eastern-central and southeastern Europe.

Srbik's monumental work seems so important because it presents in masterly form an interpretation of Austria's mission which during the last years has been accepted by many Austrians although certainly not by all.[3] The same view is also presented in a coöperative effort of Austrian scholars which was published in 1936 under the editorship of the well-known literary historian Professor Josef Nadler and of Professor Srbik. Its title, *Österreich, Erbe und Sendung im deutschen Raum*, is a program: "Austria — inheritance and mission in the German orbit." Its intention is twofold: to make the Germans in the Bismarckian Reich understand that Austria is a most important part of Germany, and to make the Austrians realize that they are nothing but an integral part of Germany. It was, after all, not so long ago that a leading German historian, Heinrich von Treitschke, could exclaim: "Denn was ist Österreich anderes als ein Fremder?" ("For what is Austria to us but alien?") The authors of the present volume all belong to the *grossdeutsch* and Pan-German tradition. The aim of creating a strongly integrated *Mittel-Europa* under undisputed German hegemony was to them the most important legacy of the war of 1914. Most characteristic and most outspoken in this respect is Reinhold Lorenz in his chapter on Austria in central Europe from 1867 to 1918. There he adopts all

---

[3] Srbik himself mentions (*Historische Zeitschrift*, CLVI, 243) that his interpretation is regarded by certain circles in Austria as a disguised Prussian interpretation, "die in unlösbarem Widerspruch zum österreichischen Staatsgedanken stehe, die österreichische Geschichte verzeichne und letzen Endes zu Gewalt und Bluttat führe" ("which represents an insoluble contradiction to the Austrian idea, misrepresents Austrian history, and will lead ultimately to the unleashing of force and the shedding of blood").

the slogans of an expansive Pan-Germanism and de-
clares with disarming naïveté (p. 176) that during the
first years of the war of 1914 a negotiated peace
(*Verständigungsfriede*) would have been possible if
France had definitely renounced Alsace-Lorraine, if
Germany had been indemnified with a restitution of
Belgium which would have taken into consideration
Germany's security, and if Germany had been given
a free hand to reorganize the non-Russian east and
southeast of Europe in such a way as to make it a
bulwark against Russian Bolshevism. Small wonder
that the non-German nationalities in the Habsburg
empire — after all, the large majority of the population — did not welcome a policy which treated them
as cannon fodder for the establishment of German
rule over all the territory, inhabited by Slavs and
others, from the Baltic to the Black and Aegean seas.

Not all the essays collected in this book are as outspoken as that by Lorenz. They make definitely
clear how much of an oversimplification it is to speak
of the mission of Austria as being within the German
orbit. Austria certainly has made her contribution,
and a most important one, to the general German
development. She could do it, however, because she
had her own destiny and mission in collaboration and
cohabitation with non-Germanic peoples and civilizations. The history of Austria can be considered as
being part of a much wider orbit than the German
orbit. Any narrowing-down of Austria to an integral
part of Germany gives a one-dimensional and distorted

perspective, at least of Habsburg Austria, from the Reformation to 1918. Such a perspective does not explain the growth or nature of Austria: it explains only her disintegration and doom from 1867 to 1918. The foundation of Austrian civilization was the Baroque, a peculiar and specific, and at the same time a universal, civilization.[4] Later on, the influences of French classicism penetrated into Austria and shaped the intention of the Habsburgs to transform their inherited lands into a dynastic Austrian state, to no longer regard them primarily as a center of the Holy Roman Empire or as a center of a German state. This idea of the Austrian state, developed by Charles VI, found its highest expression under Maria Theresa and its most sublime spiritualization in the Austrian music. The end of the eighteenth century, with new ideas penetrating into Austria from France and Germany, threw the country into a long period of change, of manifold influences penetrating from all sides, of hesitation, and of incertitude. Its national character, the foundation of which the centuries of the Baroque and of classicism had laid, is nothing definite, nothing profoundly original, but rather a fluid harmonization

---

[4] Josef Nadler gives in the volume *Österreich* (pp. 319-21) a picture of this Baroque civilization which was the foundation of a "volkhaft und sprachlich neutrale Staatsbildung. Aus dieser lateinisch-romanischen Gemeinbildung des Weltreiches erwächst auf allen Gebieten eine ebenso gemeinsame Kunst mit dem gleichen barocken Stilgepräge in Bildkunst und Baukunst, in Musik, Dichtung und Theater. . . . Weltmacht Österreich heisst Dichtung aus dem Gesamterlebnis Europas und aus dem formbildenden Willen eines grossstaatlichen Gesamtverbandes."

and acclimatization of many elements stemming from different lands and intellectual climates.

Austria, as far as she was German, created a new and different form of German civilization. She expanded its possibilities and its frame. She received most of her formative influences from the south, from the west, and from the east, and assimilated them to such a degree of perfection that out of them she created something entirely new and, at the same time, typically Austrian and unique. Vienna was not only a German city and not only the capital of the *Donauraum*: it was a European city, and its fate closely interconnected with the fate of Europe. "Austria erit in orbe ultima" was true even at a time when the great monarchy had disappeared but for a small remnant. Even this small remnant played a role for the life, peace, and happiness of Europe entirely out of proportion to its actual size. Its annexation by Germany did not inaugurate a period of a *grossdeutsch* or even *gemeindeutsch* development in the sense of a true synthesis of Berlin and Vienna, of the universal and the narrowly nationalistic. Vienna did not become a second and equal focus of German civilization. It was quickly reduced to the status of a small provincial town without special distinction. Vienna was absorbed by Berlin, a new *kleindeutsch* solution had been found — only that this time *Kleindeutschland* expanded beyond the frontiers of 1866 and 1871, to include lands which Bismarck could not reach on account of the existence of the Habsburg empire, and

the possession of which opened the ways for such an
expansion of Berlin's control and dominion as the
Bismarckian and Wilhelmian Germany could never
have hoped for. In possession of Vienna, Berlin resumed the universal tendencies of the Habsburg empire and reached out to Prague and Poland, Hungary
and Rumania, Italy and the Balkans, but on the basis
of a narrow, nationalistic militarism. The consequences for western Europe of the seizure of Vienna
will be infinitely greater and graver than the consequences of Königgrätz were for France. Austria and
the Austrian idea seemed ended at the very time when
their existence appeared necessary for the future of
German civilization as well as for the peace of Europe:
as a counterbalance against the one-sided uniformity
of all cultural life in the German Reich, against
the sacrifice of the fruitful diversity of life and of the
manifoldness of German spiritual inheritance to the
gray monotony of an armed camp; and as a nucleus
for the necessary federation of all the peoples in
eastern-central Europe, a role to which Vienna was
historically and geographically predestined, especially
after having given up the dream of hegemony and
dominion.

The *grossdeutsch* and Pan-German interpretation
of Austria's mission was, however, not accepted by all
Austrians after the war of 1914. For them even the
catastrophe of 1918 did not necessarily imply the end
of Austria or of the Austrian idea. It is true that in
1918 the liberal (the word taken in the specific Aus-

trian sense, which had its roots in Josephinism and meant anticlerical and economically progressive) educated middle classes and the social democracy turned away from the Austrian tradition and joined the Pan-Germans in the demand for a union with Germany. The opposing circles were small at the beginning — monarchists, some traditionalists, some Roman Catholics. The revolutionary catastrophe seemed at first to bury the whole past and to render it meaningless; but as time went on, and the situation in Austria began to consolidate itself, the peculiar problems of Austria and her specific traditional mission began to be reconsidered. The name of Ignaz Seipel, a militant and authoritarian cleric who paved the way for fascism in Austria, should be mentioned in this connection. In the church and among what was left of the former imperial bureaucracy and army the old traditions survived. Some Austrian writers and poets, such as Hugo von Hofmannsthal, Anton Wildgans, Josef Roth, and Ernst Krenek, represented in their works the spiritual legacy and problems of the *Homo Austriacus*.

The situation changed rapidly after 1932. The Nazification of Germany in 1933 turned many Social Democrats, liberals, and Catholics back toward Austria. The Austrian government, then under the leadership of Engelbert Dollfuss and later under that of his successor, Kurt Schuschnigg, tried now to develop an Austrian ideology, a non-Pan-Germanic interpretation of Austria's mission, founded upon the history and tradition of many centuries. Chancellor Schusch-

nigg himself has written the history of this new
Austria in a book which is a historical narration
and a personal confession at the same time.[5] "A great
Austrian and a good German," [6] the chancellor saw
in Austria the "perfect harmony of classic-humanist,
National-German, and Christian-occidental elements," a country "unique in its peculiar character,
irreplaceable in its historic and cultural values." He
saw it not only as the heir of a great imperial and
universal past but also as guarantor of the peace in
the future.

That the idea of the [supranational old Austrian] Reich
should be kept alive, though transferred to the spiritual and
cultural realm, continues to be Austria's hereditary duty,
founded on history. . . . Our new state would not be Austria, would not be worthy to exist, if its inherited mission, in
new modern form, were not capable of realization. Yet
neither force, nor arms, but rather the spirit and cultural
work, will discharge the task of mediation in an area re-
sounding with many languages, politically organized into
independent states, but which still needs both spiritually and
economically some unifying element in order to survive.
Such a service for Europe can be performed today only by
a country which does not fall under the suspicion of following imperialist aim.[7]

[5] Kurt Schuschnigg, *Dreimal Österreich* (Vienna, 1937). The
American edition appeared under the title *My Austria* (New York,
1938) and contains an introduction by Dorothy Thompson, an
index, and several illustrations, absent in the original edition.
[6] With these words the editorial in the *Neue Freie Presse*, Feb. 25,
1938, began its report on Schuschnigg's famous address of Feb. 24
before the Austrian Bundestag.
[7] Of the four quotations from Schuschnigg, the first is taken from
his address of February 24, 1938, as reported in the *Neue Freie Presse*
of the next day; the following three, from *Dreimal Österreich*, pp. 10,
20, and 22.

This interpretation of Austria's mission emphasized two aspects: the necessity of its independence for German civilization, and the necessity of its continued existence for the peace and coöperation of central Europe and even of Europe. German and human civilization will be infinitely poorer by the disappearance of that which was Austria. It was characteristic of Austria to show tolerance and moderation, to avoid all extremes, to be well-tempered, to permeate its life with a broad-minded catholicity and with a strong tendency to ease the living together of different types and races. A mellow and easy-going charm, a richness of color and music, and a balanced reasonableness made life so different from any stiff and drab uniformity, from any cutting and steely hardness. Austria was able, as Schuschnigg said, to purvey German spirit and culture to the world in such a wise as to gain not only respectful admiration but also love and personal sympathy. Austria was not only a German march, it was also a bridge, on which Germany and the smaller peoples of central Europe could meet, where all the civilizations of Europe could mingle for mutual stimulation. The multinational Reich of the Habsburgs had appeared to many as an anachronism. It was that, but it was also a promise for the future; and many former Austrians and subjects of the Habsburgs may understand the value and function of the old Austria only now that it has ceased to exist. The urgent problem before central Europe in the period between the two wars of 1914 and 1939

was the same as the Austrian problem had been at the
beginning of the twentieth century, and will be the
same after the present war — the problem of a federation of equal peoples, not in submission and uniformity, but in freedom and tolerance. In her best
moments Old Austria had shown in a very imperfect
form, as an embryonic promise, the possibility of such
a federation without brutality or domination, without any exclusiveness or exclusivism. The end of
Austria meant the end of a hope whose realization
seems more necessary to many observers today than
at any time before.

Schuschnigg's book, however, reveals also the se-
vere limitations of his personality and of the whole
Dollfuss-Schuschnigg regime. Although an Austrian
patriot, he was a fervent German nationalist, and he
was limited in his outlook by his clerical and fascist
sympathies. By the narrowness of his viewpoint and
of his education (he had been the pupil of Jesuits, of
whom he stresses, above all, the German nationalism
and Pan-German tendencies), Schuschnigg missed the
opportunity of making Austria a rallying-point of
anti-Nazi Germanism. After Hitler's accession to
power in Germany, the situation offered to Dollfuss
and Schuschnigg a great historical chance — not to
stress that Austria was German, which needed no
stressing, as nobody denied it, nor did anybody
threaten or endanger it — but to emphasize that German was not identical with National Socialist. National Socialism (not a product of the peace treaties)

had its roots, indeed, in certain aspects of the German, and especially of the Prussian, tradition. National Socialism undoubtedly is a specifically German movement, but National Socialism is in no way an expression of the whole tradition and essence of Germanism. It wipes out many of the most important sides of the more than millenary development of a nation famous for its diversity; it falsifies and reinterprets in a most arbitrary way many other sides; it may even be regarded, although specifically German, as a perversion of the German tradition. Whether this last view is tenable or not, there is no doubt that there have been and still are other sides of Germanism than those stressed by the forerunners, prophets, and philosophers of National Socialism. Austria could have developed into a conscious rallying-point of a non- and anti-National-Socialist Germanism, of one more humane, more western, "catholic," and European.

Such a united German front, in order to have the vitality and appeal to resist the revolutionary dynamism of National Socialism, would have had to take an uncompromising democratic stand. Schuschnigg could not conceive of such a synthesis of all the available forces. Seipel and his disciples had started, of their own, a violent propaganda for anti-Marxism, against democracy and liberalism, and had taken their stand with the rising forces of fascism. Having themselves gone a very long way on the same road as National Socialism, how could they oppose it, with the hope of success? Politically it might have seemed possible as long as fascist Italy and National-Socialist Germany remained brothers in spirit without becoming brothers in arms. But ideologically the difference was too small. The German nationalist position was also accepted by Seipel and his followers with regard to the war of 1914 and its sequence. A foreign policy for Austria could be imagined by them only in close coöperation with Germany. To resist National Socialism, however, it would have been necessary to represent something fundamentally different from National Socialism. For that purpose a new German cultural "axis," with its main supports in Vienna, Zürich, and Prague, was desirable — a reorientation of the foreign policy toward European coöperation and the League of Nations, and, above all, the creation of a democratic regime in Austria on a broad popular basis, embracing Socialists and Catholics, legitimists and liberals. Instead, the Dollfuss and Schuschnigg regimes followed in the wake of fascism and thereby prepared the way for *Gleichschaltung*. The treaty of July 11, 1936, with Germany softened or silenced the anti-National-Socialist propaganda in Austria and undermined the possibilities of a strong cultural anti-National-Socialist policy in the interests of a broader German civilization and of Austria's true German mission.

It should not be overlooked that the Austrian dictatorship was never fascist in the real sense of the word but was a hybrid form, and was built not upon the support of rising masses of the lower middle class or of the youthful nationalistic intelligentsia but upon some still lingering traditional forces of the recent past, adorned with some of the paraphernalia of fascism and held together by a militant clericalism. But there was none of the efficiency and ruthlessness, noisy brutality, and mechanization of life which characterize fascism. The rhythm of life and the traditions of Austria persevered; the Austrian dictatorship was much more human and humane than that of Mussolini or Hitler, disdaining all emotional mass appeal, remaining to a large extent (at least compared with fascism) rational and civilized. In its life and atmosphere in 1937, Vienna resembled a western European city much more than it resembled Berlin or Rome. But this hybrid form could not save Austria. Austria was condemned, not only by the shortsighted optimism of the democratic nations but also by the insufficiency of Schuschnigg, whose friends were the first to betray him in the hour of need. His tragic fate — when, in modern times, was the head of a defeated and annexed country held in more cruel and secret imprisonment by the victorious enemy? — shows the futility and peril of any compromise with, or any friendly inclination toward, National Socialism.

The danger and weakness of Schuschnigg's position was clearly seen by a group of Austrians of whom the Catholic sociologist Ernst Karl Winter may be regarded as representative. He regards Rudolph IV, who bears in Austrian history the title of *der Stifter* — he was the builder of St. Stephen's Cathedral, the

founder of Vienna University, the inventor of the
title "archduke," the forger of the Privilegium Maius
— as the creator of the Austrian consciousness, who
definitely loosened Austria's ties with the German
orbit and opened the road to supraracial forms of
political organization embracing the different peoples
of the Danubian area. It is interesting to note that
Dr. Winter arrives at the conclusion that Austria was
created from its Viennese center, that Vienna was the
originator of Austria, and that this primacy of the
urbs guarantees the identity of Austria, whether it be
the inheritance of the Babenberg dukes, or the Aus-
trian-Bohemian-Hungarian inheritance of 1526, or
the Austria of 1918, "a mere remnant in the eyes of
some, a European task in the vision of others." Under
Rudolph IV, Austria, "although it still kept one foot
within the German orbit, stepped out of it with the
other; it learned to regard itself as a sovereign political
entity, like the neighboring states of the Přemyslids,
Arpads, and Piasts, which all had taken this step out
of the Reich long ago, partly with papal help." The
union of Austria with Bohemia and Hungary (and
potentially even with Poland) was long pre-formed
in the policy of the Habsburgs and even of the Babenbergs, but also of the other dynasties ruling this
area. That can best be seen in the marriages and family ties which in these periods mirror the aspirations
of the states. Already the Babenbergs intermarried
mostly with the Bohemian and Hungarian houses and,
as the Arpads did, with the Byzantines. The Habs-

burgs continued to strengthen these ties in an even
more marked way, made it from the beginning the
fundamental line of their policy, more so even than
the well-known "bella gerant alii, tu, felix Austria,
nube!" implies. The three great rulers in this area in
the fourteenth century were great-grandchildren of
Rudolph von Habsburg: Rudolph IV in Austria,
through father and grandfather; Charles IV of Bohemia, through mother and grandmother; Lewis the
Great of Hungary, through father and grandmother.
The famous double wedding between the children of
Rudolph von Habsburg and Přemysl Otokar II at the
end of the thirteenth century was paralleled in the
middle of the fourteenth century in the marriages of
the two daughters of Charles IV with Rudolph IV of
Habsburg and his brother, and finally culminated in
the famous Viennese double marriage of the grand-
children of Maximilian I. The year 1526 brought only
the harvest of the policy of many centuries.

In many ways the policy of the great kings and
dukes in the Danubian area in the fourteenth century
followed parallel lines, all founded upon the consciousness of the essential unity of this area. When
the definite unity was achieved at the beginning of
the sixteenth century, the political mysticism of the
Baroque saw in the union of Austria, Bohemia, and
Hungary — in the *Monarchia Austriaca* — a parallel
to the Holy Trinity, or to the three wise kings, as
represented through their medieval saints, St. Leo-
pold, St. Stephen, and St. Wenceslas. From this point

of view Austria's heirdom and mission appear not
primarily as German but as supranational and European; its formation, with its foundations deep back
in the middle ages, and its growth not conditioned or
made possible by the connection with Germany but
by the orientation toward the other peoples and king-
doms of eastern-central Europe. Like its past, its
future is seen basically bound up not with Germany
but with the other peoples with whom the Austrians
have lived together for so many centuries and in the
contact with whom the *Homo Austriacus* developed.
In opposition to the Pan-Germanic interpretation and
vision of Heinrich Ritter von Srbik, a supranational,
Austrian, and European interpretation and vision
were attempted. Such a vision could have been shared
— and has been — by the non-Germanic peoples
who lived formerly within the Habsburg monarchy
and whose fate and destinies seem even today closely
interlinked, in spite of recent political boundaries. A
central European federation, uniting without any
hegemony or predominance many different nationalities and civilizations, could have become the image
and the kernel of a European federation. Thinking
of Austria, possibilities of the past mingle with visions
of the future. The unique history and form of the
political structure which had grown up around the
imperial city of Vienna call forth speculations which
seem to have no firm foundation in the tumultuous
reality of the last twenty-five years, and even less in
the complete chaos which spread from Germany to

the whole of central and eastern Europe through the conquest of Vienna.

There is no doubt that visions of the future and the appraisal of the situation in which Europe and civilization find themselves today have influenced also the interpretations of the past. "Austria erit in orbe ultima": Austria's fate and her end have become symbolic of Europe's destiny. But already during the lifetime of Frederick III, in 1485, an Austrian chronicler interpreted *A E I O U* as "Aller erst ist Österreich verloren" ("First of all Austria will perish"). Is the end of Austria the beginning of general chaos? In my childhood, in Austrian schools, we used to sing: "Österreich wird ewig stehn" ("Austria will stand forever"). Today Austria no longer exists. In a time of apparent general retrogression, Austria, too, seems to have obliterated centuries of development and to have reverted to her pristine position as Ostmark. In the realm of contemporary factuality, the Pan-Germanic interpretation of Austria's heirdom and mission has carried the day. But this factual solution of the hour does not necessarily imply the validity of such an interpretation or a final answer as to the future. Long-lasting historical forms which have a foundation in geographic realities sometimes reveal a strong tendency to reappear in new shapes and configurations. The enigmatic five vowels in which a Habsburg prince expressed his premonition of the future still may not have yielded the fulness of their meaning.

II

Czech Democracy

THE nineteenth century regarded liberal democracy with its parliamentary representative institutions, its equality of all citizens before the law, and its respect of inalienable individual rights and liberties, as an attitude which was destined to become common to all mankind. The events of that century, culminating in the victory of the liberal democratic powers in the first world war and in the ensuing democratization of the whole planet, seemed to bear out this conviction. At the beginning of the twentieth century society had been organized on progressively democratic lines — even in the Far East, in Turkey, and in Latin America. The year 1918 accelerated the development. The old conservative monarchies were everywhere swept away, republics constituted, and suffrage extended to all. The ideals which had moved the peoples in their spring in 1848 seemed now realized; in a fall seventy years later a bountiful harvest was reaped. But in many cases this harvest was premature; there had been no sufficient period of growth. Thus it is not surprising that new forces arose, denying democracy and the progressive ideals of the nineteenth century. These new forces were no longer half-hearted and partly apologetic like the anti-liberal movement in the nineteenth century; they did not remain on the defensive, drawing their inspiration from the *ancien régime*. They were aggressive, prose-lytizing, with an exuberant faith in their own future. Liberal democracy, east of the Rhine and of the Alps, could nowhere withstand the tremendous pressure of these new forces. This was not only true of nations which preserved their aristocratic structure — where the national movement had taken shape under aristo-cratic leadership — as with the Germans, the Poles, and the Hungarians. It became true even of peoples whose whole structure was democratic, who had lost their aristocracy by extermination or by assimilation, and whose national movements had been shaped by a middle class rising from peasant stock, as with the Bulgarians, the Ukrainians, the Slovaks, and the Baltic peoples. The only exception to this general trend was presented by the Czechs. Sociologically they resem-bled the peasant peoples; practically all leaders of their national movement were from the lower or lowest classes, sometimes — like Masaryk or Beneš — directly from peasant stock, sometimes only one generation removed from peasant origin. The Czechs had an aristocracy among whom some felt patriotically Czech, but it played no role in the national renais-sance. As regards the sociological foundations for democracy, the Czechs resembled other peoples in eastern Europe for whom the nineteenth century brought the awakening from a long slumber and a reintroduction into history. But only with the Czechs was this sociological foundation strengthened by a philosophy of democracy, which was based upon an interpretation of Czech history and became part, by pervading the whole of Czech education, of the mental and moral inheritance of the nation.

Democracy can develop vigorously only if supported and inspired by historical tradition, embodied in conspicuous works and deeds. This function is fulfilled in the United States by the Bill of Rights and the Declaration of Independence, as well as in the lives and thoughts of men like Thomas Jefferson and Abraham Lincoln; in England in the Magna Charta, in the revolutions of the seventeenth century, in the struggle for the reform of Parliament, in the works and lives of Milton, Locke, and Gladstone; in France by the enlightenment of the eighteenth century and by the revolutions of 1789, 1830, and 1848. Historical facts and examples grow into social myths which are closely woven into the whole texture of national life. Historiography frequently plays a great role in this process. The interpretation of the national past serves as an answer to the question about the meaning and the destiny of the national existence of a people, as a symbol around which the national cultural life is integrated and which determines the vision of the future.

These symbols express and to a certain extent determine the national character; they shape the ways of the people and the mood of its literature. Their importance should not be underestimated. It was the

tragedy of the Weimar Republic that it did not understand how to create a new symbol for the German
people as a new foundation for its faith in itself and
its mission. By its preparation for *revanche*, by its
elevation of the imperial marshal to the highest
civilian office, it left the symbol intact which from
the times of Frederick II and Bismarck had progressively determined German life; namely, the belief in
the invincibility and in the moral example of the
Prussian army. In the shaping of these symbols historians played a great role. Tragic consequences for
Germany and for Europe were involved in Bismarck's
success and in the fact that German leading historians either were strictly conservative or glorified
the preëminence of the militarist and monarchical
state over the liberal and democratic attitudes of western Europe. As the victory of 1870 definitely raised
Bismarck to the rank of a national hero, so it seemed
to confirm the tenets of the school of Prussian historians about the superiority, even the moral superiority, of conservative monarchism over liberalism.
The Weimar Republic did not produce a reinterpre-
tation of German history; thus this brief interlude
was followed by an intensification of the tendencies
which had dominated German historiography from
romanticism to Treitschke. On the other hand, a long
line of French historians, from Lamartine and Michelet on, played a decisive role in determining the outlook of the French people on the French Revolution
and its own past, and thereby its conceptions of its
future and of its place in the world.

What was accomplished in other cases by a number of historians was accomplished among the Czechs by one man, František Palacký (1798–1876), who was much more than the first great Czech historian. He has been called the Father of the Nation, the first of the national awakeners; he certainly can claim to have been the national educator. He helped to create Czech national consciousness by lending to Czech history a meaning which dignified the past by a proud and inspiring vision and justified the hard struggle which the Czechs had to make for their national renaissance. He gave to the Czechs the sense of a mission, a *raison d'être* for the aspiration to take anew their place on the field of history. His interpretation of the Czech past created the secure foundation for Czech democracy; it became a living intellectual tradition, vitalizing all manifestations of Czech life.

Palacký was the father of modern Czech nationalism. The age of enlightenment had witnessed, in the second half of the eighteenth century, the rise of a new feeling of patriotism; but this new feeling, which expressed itself largely in learned and antiquarian enterprises, was no Czech nationalism: it was a Bohemian patriotism which did not look for its foundation in the Czech people, but in the territorial entity of Bohemia and its historical traditions founded upon the rights and privileges of the Bohemian Estates. This patriotism could be common to all peoples living in Bohemia, Czechs and Germans alike. It was much removed from any nationality demands in the modern sense of the word. It could be compared to the Irish patriotism of those Protestant landlords in Ireland who in the second half of the eighteenth century insisted upon the rights and privileges of the Irish nation, of the Irish parliament; a patriotism of a purely constitutional and even English character, worlds apart from any Gaelic nationalism or any identification with the Catholic Gaelic people of Ireland as opposed to the English. In this eighteenth-century patriotism, an insistence upon historical privileges was tied up with the emphasis of the eighteenth-century enlightenment upon education, facilitated so much in the Habsburg lands by the benevolent and progressive policy of Maria Theresa and especially of Joseph II.

It was Palacký who provided the rising Czech nationalism, a product of the influences of the French Revolution and of German romanticism, with a firm foundation. He created for the Czechs a distinct idea of their own, an idea which explained and integrated their history, and at the same time distinguished them from and opposed them to the Germans. Under the existing geographic and historical circumstances, Czech national consciousness could develop only by comparison with and contrast to the Germans in whose midst the Czechs had lived politically, economically, and culturally. Palacký replaced the Bohemian patriotism of the Estates by a Czech nationalism of the people and gave the Czechs a national *raison d'être*. Thus he solved also a problem which preoccupied him and his disciple Masaryk, the problem of the right of small nations, of the desirability of and necessity for the renaissance of small nations. Palacký was too deeply steeped in the moral philosophy of Kant to derive the rights of a small nation from its mere existence or to justify it merely politically or vitalistically; for him rights must be based upon moral and cultural foundations. And Palacký already anticipated, in the middle of the last century, the progressive unification of mankind as the result of technical and economic developments; he was convinced that the time of small states had passed and that mankind was driven irresistibly towards the creation of very large political and economic units, and even towards world organization. Thus for him a small people could exist only on the strength of its intellectual and moral achievements. "Whenever we were victorious," he used to remind the Czechs, "it was always more as the result of spiritual forces than of physical might, and whenever we succumbed, there was always the insufficiency of our spiritual activity and of our moral courage responsible for it." If the Czechs wished to exist they must not only equal their neighbors, spiritually and morally, but surpass them.

Palacký created his symbol of Czech national consciousness by reinterpreting Czech history. During the two hundred years from the Battle of White Mountain (1620) to the publication of the first volume of his *Geschichte von Böhmen* (1836),[1] Bo-

---

[1] It is interesting to note that Palacký wrote his great history in German, but characteristically changed the title for the Czech edi-

hemian historiography, under the influence of the victorious Counter Reformation, had regarded Bohemia as a whole as an integral part of the Catholic world and had therefore condemned the Hussites and the Bohemian Brethren as heretic revolutionists against this world, as promoters of a deplorable madness responsible for the devastation of Bohemia, for her isolation from the general currents of Europe, for the decline of the Czechs, and ultimately for their defeat in 1620. Palacký, who came himself of a Protestant family, rehabilitated the Hussites; to a certain extent his interpretation can be compared to the rehabilitation of Cromwell and the Puritan Revolution by Carlyle after the treatment they had suffered in the historiography of the Restoration and the eighteenth century. The ethos underlying Carlyle's historiography was fundamentally different from that inspiring Palacký, however. The Czech historian found in the Czech Reformation the culmination and the meaning of Czech history, whose decisive period began with Jan Hus and the Hussite movement and experienced its last and most sublime flowering in the Bohemian Brethren. This interpretation determined not only the character of Czech history and of the Czech mission, but also the relations of the Czechs to the Germans and to Europe generally.

---

tion from "History of Bohemia" to *Dějiny národu českého* ("History of the Czech Nation"). The last volume appeared in 1876, shortly before Palacký's death. The first volume of the Czech edition was published, appropriately enough, in the March of 1848, the spring of the peoples.

We can trace clearly in Palacký the several influences which determined his attitude.[2] The first of them was that of the French Enlightenment. He accepted from it on the one hand its deep liberalism, its respect of individual rights, its optimistic faith in progress, and on the other hand its dislike of the Middle Ages and its scant interest in theological dogmatic speculations. Although he was a deeply religious man, his religion bore the character of the humanitarian theism of the eighteenth century, not that of the speculative fervor of seventeenth-century transcendentalism. From Kant, who may be regarded as the philosophical consummation of western enlightenment in Germany, he accepted the fundamental thesis that men must always put the good of mankind and scientific truth above the nation's interests, and that political life must be governed by the same moral rules as private life. From romanticism and Hegel, Palacký learned the fundamental conception that history and life are struggle, and that their development proceeds under the law of contradiction, or, as he called it frequently, polarity. Eighteenth-century enlightenment had stressed the elements of unity and harmony in the world and their growth with the progress of time; the nineteenth century emphasized the elements of struggle and conflict, later even glorified life as heroic struggle. Palacký in 1848 shared

[2] There is no satisfactory study on Palacký in English or in German. In Czech we have, in addition to a number of other important studies, the comprehensive work by Josef Fischer, *Myšlenka a dílo Františka Palackého* (2 vols., Prague, 1926–27).

the cosmopolitan enthusiasm of his generation, children of the late eighteenth century. Later on he grew more and more conservative, more and more nationalistic, and more and more cautious in his hopes for the future. He never abandoned the faith in natural rights and in *die humane Bestimmung* which had characterized him as an "eighteen-forty-eighter," but in his political and cultural utterances he became more and more reactionary — a determined opponent of general suffrage, of complete political equality, of socialism; anti-semitic; and stressing, on the other hand, more and more the importance of aristocracy and even of the Catholic Church. Nevertheless, in his historiography he continued to regard history as a struggle of ideas, of ethico-religious conceptions, and in this struggle, which was for him the essence of history, he claimed for the Czechs the honor of having been the first fighters for human freedom and for liberal democracy.

Considering history as being a struggle of two opposite principles, Palacký saw the Germans and the Slavs as the representatives of the two opposed tendencies. Herein he followed a general trend of the time. The outline of the scheme had been proposed by Herder and accepted and overworked by the Russian Slavophiles. The famous Královedvorský and Zelenohorský manuscripts which Václav Hanka claimed to have discovered in 1817 and published in 1818 seemed to furnish historical proof for the picture which Palacký and the Slav romanticists drew of early Slav civilization. Palacký never doubted the authenticity of these manuscripts, which only after his death were definitely established as forgeries. He regarded the Slavs as a people approaching the Rousseau ideal, pious, peace-loving, close to nature, gaining their livelihood by hard labor as peasants and shepherds. The Germans represented the opposite ideal; they were bellicose and well organized under competent leadership, trying to gain their livelihood, not by peaceful work, but by conquest and by obliging the vanquished to work for their lords. The Slavs lived in a primitive democracy where classes and castes were unknown and all were equal. But they loved liberty too much to subject themselves to authority and thus to create a strong and durable state; their communities inclined towards anarchy and suffered from a lack of leadership and organization. Thus they became an easy prey to their stronger and more progressive neighbors. This picture was common to the Russian Slavophiles, the Polish Messianists, and Palacký; but only Palacký drew from it a conclusion which made the Czechs the protagonists of freedom and democracy in their more developed stages. The Slavophiles stressed an authoritarian order and glorified the Orthodox church, the Polish Messianists accepted the Catholic and aristocratic tradition of Poland; only Palacký stressed and proclaimed the Protestant and liberal character of the Czech struggle against the Germans.

For him the essence and meaning of Czech history

was the opposition between the Czechs and the Germans — not in the sense of political struggle, and certainly not in the sense of war-like conflict, but rather a differentiation based upon moral ideas and national psychologies. Roughly, it may be said that the Germans represented the authoritarian and aristocratic, the Czechs the liberal and democratic, principles. This opposition culminated in the Hussite movement, which originated according to Palacký in a typically Czech interpretation of Christianity. He underestimated the medieval character of the movement; he saw in it the beginning of modern Europe, the first definite blow against the Middle Ages with their spiritual authoritarianism and their feudal structure of society. The Czech people in the Hussite Wars pioneered for the whole of humanity in a spiritual struggle for freedom of conscience, for the equality of men, against authority and hierarchy. Of course, the Hussites were in no way modern men; but their fight contained the seeds out of which later a freer and more humane Europe grew up. The Hussite Revolution not only started the Protestant Reformation, but carried the germs for the future growth of rationalism and freedom of thought, of democracy and socialism, on a basis of religious idealism, of nationalism, and of the new spirit of activity pervading the masses. In the Hussite movement, with its ethical rigorism and its chiliastic enthusiasm, he saw the forerunner of the Puritan revolution, which in its turn heralded the American and the French revolutions.

That the Czechs could fulfill this function in history Palacký explained by the facts that the level of education had been higher in Bohemia — especially under Charles IV — than in any of the surrounding countries, that feudalism and serfdom had not yet fully been established among the Czechs, and that with the more intense intellectual life the old Slavonic democracy and liberty lived on. The old opposition of Slav democracy and German aristocracy was resumed on a higher level under the religious inspiration of Hussitism, and became of world-wide importance.

Palacký explained the breakdown of Hussitism and with it the decay of the Czech people by the fact that by the end of the fifteenth century the aristocratic feudal principle had gained the upper hand in Bohemia; serfdom was introduced in 1487. Outside of the movement of the Bohemian Brethren, which continued and purified the Hussite attitude, Hussitism itself tended to turn into an oppressive orthodoxy. Whereas Bohemia retrogressed, the seeds of the new humanism which the Hussites had sown began to bear fruit in the progress of the world outside Bohemia, where the free spirit of the old Slavonic democracy disappeared. The Czechs had undertaken the great task of the liberation of the human spirit from medieval authority too early; as forerunners they could not reap the harvest themselves. The German and Swiss reformation, the Puritans, eighteenth-century rationalism, the French Revolution, all continued, deepened, and amplified what the Czechs had begun. The Czechs themselves succumbed to the power of Rome and Spain; the Hussite past became in their own eyes heretical and damnable. The Czech catastrophe was due to the desertion by the Czechs of their own democratic ideals, to the oppression of the common people and its ensuing lethargy. The emancipation of the peasants under Emperor Joseph II and the improvement of their economic and educational situation made possible the Czech renaissance of the nineteenth century, which Masaryk declared to be directly linked to the Czech reformation and to be similarly an ethico-religious movement.

Thus Palacký endowed the Czech people with the consciousness of the identification of the Czech cause with that of democracy. The Hussites had fought for the liberty of conscience and for democratic equality against the authoritarianism of Rome and the bellicose feudalism of the Germans. Their movement was ethico-religious, national, and social at the same time. Hus, like Luther, fought against Rome. German national historiography sometimes interpreted Luther's reformation as the first great act of national emancipation, as Palacký regarded the Hussite movement. But in Luther's reformation the democratic and liberal elements in which Palacký saw the core of Hussitism were entirely lacking. In spite of the fact that Czech nationalism found its expression in a moral and ideological opposition to what could be called the German idea, Palacký always rejected

an interpretation of the relations of the Slavs and
Germans as hammer and anvil. He opposed German
rule over the Slavs, but he repudiated any idea of Slav
domination over the Germans. In the epilogue of his
Gedenkblätter, two years before his death, he found
it necessary to defend himself against the many attacks
directed against him for his conciliatory attitude
towards the Germans and Austrians: "Trust in humanity and in the love of the Germans for justice:
who will be the first to cast a stone at me for that?
Or should I even today be ashamed for that?" He
welcomed the voluntary union of the Czech and Austrian lands under Habsburg rule in 1526, because it
put an end to the possible conflicts of the different
neighboring peoples. He was by no means looking
forward eagerly to political independence for small
peoples. He believed instead in their coöperation
within larger federations. At the time of the Polish
revolution in 1863 he took an entirely realistic attitude. He blamed the Poles for not having emanci-
pated their serfs and for not having improved the lot
of the peasantry within the nation, and he advised
the Polish patriots to devote themselves to the cultural and social development of their own masses
instead of aiming at the impossible goal of Polish
independence, which would either subject non-Polish
populations to the Polish rule or leave Poland at the
mercy of her stronger neighbors. Thus he repeated
fourteen years later a conviction which he had expressed on March 21, 1849, when he wrote against

the "dream" of political independence of the Magyars and the Czechs, of the Serbs and the Rumanians. He always stressed the need of association of the smaller peoples in view of what he called the centralization or progressive unification of the whole globe.[3] He did not see in political independence a panacea. The Czechs had had political independence and had lost it. What was needed, according to Palacký, to make the Czechs a strong national organism, was a more intense cultural life, a juster social order, a greater devotion to the true spirit of Czech democracy as embodied in the Czech reformation. This emphasis upon the lasting character of Czech history and destiny gave to Czech democracy the foundation which made it independent of changing currents of thought or of shifting historical situations in the neighboring countries.

Not only did Palacký give to the Czech people

[3] Palacký said in his speech of August 27, 1861, in the House of Lords: "The Magyars and the Czechs are equally forced by destiny to join politically in a larger state and to accept the conditions of life of this larger state." T. G. Masaryk pointed out rightly in his *Palackého idea národa českého* (Prague, 1926, p. 42 f.) that "the conviction that the Czech people cannot become politically independent is one of the fundamental political conceptions of Palacký." The Czechs did not lose their national existence in 1526 by the union with Austria, as Palacký knew very well. But it is doubtful even whether the Battle of White Mountain in 1620 can be regarded as the defeat of Czech nationalism. In that battle the Habsburg prince defeated a Bohemian king who was a German. It is an open question whether the Czechs, if they had remained Protestants, would not have come very strongly under German and Prussian influences and would not have been closely incorporated into Germanic life, whereas in the non-nationalistic Habsburg state they escaped the fate of Germanization more easily.

an interpretation of their history which supported their democratic program of the present and the future by its foundations in the past. Through him the question of Czech freedom and Czech national development became indissolubly linked with the world problem of democracy. Through him Czech history became of importance for the history of Europe, the Czech question, a universal question. By regarding the rise of modern Europe and the French Revolution as fundamentally identical with the ideas of the Czech reformation, the Czechs found their place in modern Europe on the side of the great and progressive democratic currents and peoples. Their struggle against the Germans for national self-preservation became a struggle for democracy and that means for a better world and for more humane relations of all peoples. Under these circumstances Palacký's great disciple, T. G. Masaryk, could declare "the problems of humanity a specifically Czech problem." [4] Masaryk saw rightly that Palacký had not only educated the Czech people to democracy, but that he had established in the eyes of Europe the Hus-

[4] T. G. Masaryk, *The Making of a State* (New York, 1927, pp. 59 and 479 ff.). Masaryk stresses several times the importance of Palacký for him and for the Czech people. So on page 29, "Inasmuch as my political outlook was derived from Palacký"; on page 472, "My guide and master was Palacký, the Father of the Fatherland, who gave us the philosophical history of our nation, understood its place in the world and defined our national objective"; and especially on page 373, where he says that during the World War at Prague "Palacký's writings were sold out. Thinking people immersed themselves in his national program and in the testament of the Father of the Nation — an eloquent proof of political maturity."

site Reformation as the most valid Czech title to recognition. The Czech question, the question of Czech existence, had been in the past essentially "the question of religion and of humanity." It was again in the twentieth century indissolubly linked with the question of democracy, not only for the Czechs, but for Europe and for mankind. By the recent subjugation of the Czechs the Germans dealt, not accidentally, a decisive blow to world democracy.

At the beginning of the fifteenth century the ideals upon which modern civilization was founded were first proclaimed, so Palacký taught the Czechs, by the Czechs themselves in a new interpretation of Christian thought and life. The Czechs were the first to fight for these new ideals and to orientate their national life in accordance with them. Five centuries later, when the ideals of modern civilization seemed to triumph everywhere, the Czechs were able to build their existence, under the leadership of Palacký's disciple, Masaryk, the Liberator of the Czech nation, on these principles which they derived not only from the example of western Europe but from their own national traditions which antidated the former. Twenty years later, when modern civilization, as the result of the lack of foresight, courage, and coöperation on the part of its defenders, seemed to recede before the onslaught of a new barbarism, the foundations upon which Czech national life rested collapsed. The resurrection of Czech national life is bound up, as Palacký and Masaryk have foreseen, with the reassertion of those principles of human liberty and of rational humanism which, according to the Father and to the Liberator of the Czech nation, have formed the backbone of Czech history and the justification for Czech national existence.

ILLUSION AND DISILLUSION

For yourselves know perfectly that the day of the Lord so cometh as a thief in the night.

For when they shall say, Peace and safety; then sudden destruction cometh upon them, as travail upon a woman with child; and they shall not escape.

But ye, brethren, are not in darkness, that that day should overtake you as a thief. . . .

Therefore let us not sleep as do others; but let us watch and be sober.

The First Epistle of Paul to the Thessalonians, v, 2–6.

Illusion and Disillusion

LESS than five years ago, in the spring of 1936, the Emperor of Ethiopia, still fighting a desperate battle in his native country against the aggressive forces of fascism, sent out a last-minute appeal to the democratic nations to come to his help. He pointed out that if this help should not come or should come too tardily, not only would Ethiopia be lost, but with it the independence of many other countries and the foundations of Western civilization. The appeal of the Emperor remained unheeded; he had to go into exile, his country was occupied and enslaved by the fascists. What had happened then seemed to most people in the democratic countries a minor war in distant East Africa, a calamity to an uncivilized Negro people, without any importance or consequence for the future of Nordic Europe or that of the western hemisphere. Not many, if any, would then have thought that within a very few years the monarchs of Norway and the Netherlands would follow their black colleague into exile, that the governments of Denmark, Belgium, and France would be captives in their own countries, and that all these lands would be occupied and enslaved by fascist forces. The appeal sent out in the spring of 1936 by the Emperor of Ethiopia has since been reëchoed by the heads of many governments which remained firmly convinced of their impregnable safety until the very hour of their destruction had sounded.

In the fall of 1939 many Americans pointed confidently to the neutrality of the Scandinavian countries as an example to be followed by nations wishing to escape from the disaster of war. Scandinavia's neutrality had come through the first World War intact. A long tradition of neutrality and of pacifism animated these peoples, who for centuries had kept aloof from any imperialist ventures and from any entanglements. They believed in minding their own business and devoting themselves to building up a more perfect democracy through the solution of their internal problems. Although their peoples and governments had desired nothing more than to stay out of war and had done their utmost to observe the most scrupulous neutrality, Denmark and Norway lost their liberty in the first year of the war and Sweden is in mortal danger of being completely subjected to German control.

No more than the Scandinavians had the peoples and the governments of Great Britain and France desired war: the governments, above all, had dreaded the war, from which they expected no gain. They had been afraid of the possibility of social upheavals and of the certain deterioration in the status of the wealthy classes which any major war in our day involves. The governments of these two countries, under the leadership of Mr. Chamberlain, had worked unceasingly for peace; their efforts at appeasement had been criticized by many Americans who *at that*

time looked upon the international situation with foresight, courage, and some understanding of the real
nature and aims of fascism.

The policy of appeasement, which led step by step
throughout the fateful decade of the thirties to the
present situation, was not the work of Mr. Chamberlain alone and did not originate in any evil intention.
It was a policy backed by the overwhelming majority
of the democratic peoples who wished to be spared
even the risk of the ordeal of war. All classes shared
in this policy. Most representatives of high finance
and of big business, whom an obsolete cliché used to
accuse of inciting to war, backed appeasement as enthusiastically as many socialists and labor men who
opposed any thoroughgoing armament and regarded
war as an instrument of imperialism. To the civilized
and peace-loving peoples and their leaders in the democracies, the new — or, if one likes, old — interpretation of history and of the role of men underlying
fascism seemed something so fantastic that they refused to believe it or to take it seriously. The optimism and rationalism predominant in the nineteenth
century made people forget that there is evil in the
world. They comforted themselves by the illusion
that by the denial of the existence of evil, one can
destroy evil; that by looking away from evil, evil
will disappear, or by some miracle will at least be
stopped from spreading. This illusionary optimism
was at the root of the disaster which befell democratic nations.

The well-intentioned policy of appeasement in

England and France was motivated by two principal illusions in addition to a very sincere sympathy and liking for the German people on the part of the English leaders. The first illusion was well voiced by Mr. Chamberlain when he said, "War wins nothing, cures nothing, ends nothing." He forgot that throughout history wars have settled most important issues; sometimes wrongly, sometimes rightly, depending upon the point of view. But most wars in history shaped and changed the conditions under which men were to live. It is true that the democratic peoples did not wish to win anything by the war; they forgot that wars may defend something and that this something may seem worth defending: not only the independence of one's country, but also the whole tradition of freedom and of liberal life. Out of their own failure to comprehend the nature and true aims of fascism, the democratic nations find themselves fighting with their backs to the wall, not only for themselves but for human decency and liberty, when with a little more courage and farsightedness they could have saved themselves and their ways of life and values in preceding years, without bringing upon themselves and upon other peoples immense sufferings and perils.

The second illusion dominating many minds until very recently was the belief that National Socialist actions were to be explained by the fact that Germany had been wronged by the treaty of Versailles, and that some restitution was due to her. In this light, the annexation of Austria and of the Sudetenland and the remilitarization of the Rhineland were excused and even approved, except for the methods employed, by large sections of public opinion in the democracies. They did not understand that National Socialism was not out to "liberate" the Austrians or the Sudeten Germans, but that these acts constituted only steppingstones for further conquests which would lead Germany to a dominating position in the world and impose the fascist way of life upon democratic and peace-loving nations. This complete lack of comprehension of the new dynamic and world-revolutionary forces in National Socialism was at the root of the policy of appeasement and of the policy of neutrality pursued by large and small democracies of both hemispheres in a world in which the rising and exuberant forces of fascism had proclaimed a life-and-death struggle against democracy everywhere. Their confidence in the ultimate and totalitarian victory of fascism on this globe was bolstered by the confusion and illusions paralyzing the mind and morale of democracy at the very hour when it had to meet the supreme test of a new and unexpected mortal danger.

This danger arises from the fact that the present war is neither a war between Germany and other countries nor a war between two imperialisms. Of course all these issues are involved in the present war; but they only serve to obscure the fundamental reality of the conflict. Certainly there is a British imperialism as well as a French, Dutch, or American imperialism, but the identity of the word imperialism should not obliterate the fact that the imperialism of the democratic countries has little in common with the new fascist imperialism. All imperialism contains elements of ruthlessness, brutality, and exploitation. But when democratic nations are ruthless in their colonies, voices of strong protest are raised in the motherland, and the situation is generally remedied. After acting ruthlessly from time to time, democratic governments, especially the British, have always sought the road of compromise: offering concessions, trying to find some way of arrangement. The reason is simple. Brutality and the desire for ruthless domination seem unfortunately inherent in man's nature, and citizens of a democracy can be as brutal as fascists. But with the democratic peoples this brutality is controlled by a philosophy of life, by a faith, by their standards of value — whether we call it Christianity, or humanism, or liberalism. Englishmen and Americans are brutal because they do not live up to their philosophy of life; fascists are brutal because their philosophy glorifies hard ruthlessness and domination by force and rejects the notions of charity, the faith in the dignity of every individual and in the equality of all men. Liberal imperialism is the result of the weakness and defection of men who do not live up to their own ideals; fascist imperialism is the result of a proud application of the "new ideals and values"; the first might be criticized as a failure, the second has to be praised as a logical consummation.

No protest was heard in Italy against the inhuman treatment which Marshal Graziani meted out to the Arabs in Lybia; neither is any heard in Germany against the rule to which the Poles are being subjected, which has no parallel in modern European history. Liberal imperialism, often even unwillingly and unwittingly, educated the subject peoples for freedom and nurtured in them the aspirations and hopes of national liberty and unity, of the rights of the individual, of equal justice for all. Great Britain brought to the Orient the tradition of the long struggle for liberty and human dignity which has characterized English history for more centuries than the history of any other nation and which is represented by the names of Milton and Locke, of John Stuart Mill and of Gladstone. Similarly republican France carried with her the ideas of 1789 and of 1848, the glorious years of French history; and American imperialism could not unfold its flag without recalling the Declaration of Independence and the Bill of Rights. All this influenced and shaped the minds of the native peoples and awakened them from their age-old lethargy to new moral and political life.

The fascist governments, ruling subject peoples, carry with them the gospel of the inequality of men, the glorification of war and of domination. They cannot and they do not wish to awaken moral energies in the subject peoples, they throw them back into lethargy, making of them mere tools, devoid of will and aspirations. in the hands of the master race.

Fascist imperialism represents the rebirth of a much older concept of imperialism, of the period before any belief in human rights had developed, before the exercise of naked power was checked by humanitarian considerations. A fascist victory does not mean the imposition of a "dictated" peace, but the complete annihilation of the enemy nation and new forms of personal slavery for the defeated, as in ancient times.

As this war is not merely a conflict between two imperialisms, so it is not only a war between Germany and Great Britain. War in our time is fundamentally different from the wars of the nineteenth century which ended in the first world war. That war was the culmination and consummation of the wars and aspirations of the nineteenth century; at the same time it contained the germs for the new wars of the twentieth century. The second world war is, in its most important aspects, not any more a national war; it is a revolutionary war, cutting across national and racial boundaries, a civil war on a planetarian scale, conducted not only and not even mainly by means of armed conflict and after due declaration of war. The dividing lines go through all nations and races, in most cases even through the heart and mind of every man. In this conflict between world fascism and world democracy certain nations, by reason of their historical development and their strength and size, have assumed, or have been put into, the leadership of the two warring camps. National Socialist Germany is actively supported not only by totalitarian powers like Italy, Japan, and Spain — which, acting under the obsession of a legendary past and of a heroic imperial mission, are striving to realize the almost mystical dynamism animating their ruling class and enflaming the minds of their youth in a "new order" in the Mediterranean, in the Pacific, and in the Southern Atlantic — but also by the sympathy of many individuals in the democratic countries. As the hopes of the fascist-minded of all nations and races center in Berlin, so the hopes of all the democratically minded center more and more in Washington.

The failure to recognize the true character of the war has been the most powerful help for the fascist cause. This war was made possible not only by the military and psychological unpreparedness of all democracies, but also by the division of opinion in their ranks. Many people have fallen victim to the subtle fascist propaganda, which in the most dextrous way used half truths and played upon the longings for peace and the generous impulses of the democracies. Many liberals asking themselves, "Why should we fight for Ethiopians or Czechs or English?" or "Why should we send our soldiers abroad to defend distant causes?" did not realize that the fascists, in striking at Ethiopia, China, Austria, Spain, and Great Britain, aimed at countries far beyond their immediate victims. Great and small democracies continued in the illusion of an isolationism justified in the nineteenth century but obsolete in the middle of the twentieth century. The great successes of the fascist powers were built, not upon their intrinsic strength, but upon the illusions of the democracies which waited, or still are waiting, until cornered or faced by superior strength. The immense, and ten years ago unexpected, successes of fascism have made it impregnable from within, increased its self-confidence and daring, and won allies for it among all the many who are easily impressed by success.

In this confused illusionism many people asked themselves the question whether the British government headed by Mr. Chamberlain was fighting for democracy. This question was as much beside the point as a similar question would be if the United States were involved in the war. In defending themselves the democratic peoples are fighting for their democratic way of life. More important, however, is the fact that the fascist leaders know very well, and proclaim openly and loudly, that this is on their part a war against democracy everywhere. This war is an ideological war, not because Mr. Chamberlain wished it to be — he did not wish it —but because the other side fights it as an ideological war, because it derives its immense enthusiasm and its high morale from this consciousness; because its youth knows itself as the messenger of a new order, the new fascist order of mankind, which can only exist and feel safe if democracy is destroyed everywhere. The fascists are looking towards the future; in the democracies many remain fascinated by the immediate past, unable to adjust their thought-processes to the new and entirely

unforeseen situation. Thus the French general staff
entered this war fascinated by the example of the first
World War; thus the Latin-Americans regard Yankee
imperialism still as the great danger that it was twenty
years ago, and easily fall victim to the now infinitely
greater danger of fascist imperialism; thus many
people in the United States still think in the notions
and emotions aroused in the first World War.

The confused illusionism of the democracies has
been heightened by communist propaganda. The
communists, who until August 23, 1939, had vituper-
ated against the British and French governments for
not going to war against National Socialist Germany,
suddenly after this date, when Great Britain and
France did go to war, accepted the fascist thesis that
this war is a war between two imperialisms. The pact
between the National Socialist and Soviet governments was, like the neutrality legislation of the United
States, the green-light signal given to Chancellor
Hitler in the summer of 1939 for the launching of his
plans of conquest. Probably Stalin, in concluding his
agreement with the German government, committed
the same error which the Polish dictator Pilsudski had
made when he signed in January 1934 the treaty of
friendship with Germany. Probably in both cases
similar fears, hopes, and suspicions were at work. The
leaders of Poland and of the Soviet Union distrusted
the willingness and readiness of the Western powers
to fight National Socialist Germany and suspected
them of a wish to settle their differences with Ger-

many at the expense of some Eastern deal; they were afraid of an open conflict with the powerful war-machine of Germany, and they expected to reap at least temporary gains out of a prudent policy of aloofness. However that may be, the communist propaganda after August 1939 no longer turned its guns against fascism, but against democracy, and became a powerful weapon in increasing the moral and intellectual confusion in the democratic countries. Its policy thus played into Hitler's hands, as Colonel Beck had done in the five years following January 1934. The Soviet Union, as a non-belligerent, supported National Socialist Germany diplomatically, economically, and above all morally; at the same time the communists proclaimed it a crime for democratic nations, as non-belligerents, to support economically, diplomatically, and above all morally, the democratic nations so far involved in the war.

The illusions under which many people in the democracies labor are partly caused by the disillusionment which took hold of public opinion in the democracies after the World War. It is an error to make the peace treaties after the first world war responsible for the second world war. The source of the trouble lies in the fact that the promises of the peace were never executed: immediately after their victory, the democratic nations started again the old game of disunion, jealousy, and mutual distrust; France did not receive the security to which she was entitled; Americans and Britons withdrew into isolation; the League of Nations, which alone could have established a lasting peace, did not become a strong and living reality. That the "war to end war" did not end wars is not the fault of the peace treaties; the democratic peoples deserted the hopes which had animated them during the later part of the first world war.

But even this failure should not have given rise to disillusionment. This disillusionment offered an easy escape from thinking courageously and open-mindedly about the causes of the failure. It opened the way on the one hand to a cheap cynicism which denied all spiritual values and tried to "unmask" all ideals as simple pretexts for economic greed and power struggle, thus creating a vacuum in the souls of the younger generation which laid them wide open to fascist influence, and on the other hand to an easy sentimentalism which turned the brains and hearts away from the hard road of toil and sacrifice to wishful dreaming. But this disillusionment, which has been a major obstacle to any real improvement, was not justified. The ideal of a League of Nations was too young in 1919 to have gained a firm hold over the mind and imagination of the peoples. When the war broke out in 1914, nobody in all the belligerent countries thought or spoke of collective security, of making the world safe for democracy, or of a war to end war. No thought of a new international order inspired the fighters in the first years of the first world war. It was only in 1916 and 1917 that the war changed its aspect; that the people in Great Britain and France, in the United States and in the Russia of the February Revolution, began to envisage a new international order without wars; that their leaders evolved the entirely new and daring concept of a League of Nations and of international solidarity. It would have been a miracle if only a few months later these new ideas had been strong enough to overcome the old emotions and notions which in 1914 had held undisputed sway everywhere.

In this respect war in our time bears no resemblance to the first World War. Whatever the outcome of the present war, a war which started in 1936 and the end of which may not be determined by the outcome of the present struggle between Great Britain and Germany alone, there is no doubt that a return to the *status quo* of 1939 is unthinkable, politically as well as socially. At the end of the war the world will be entirely changed, not only in the belligerent countries but in every country all over the earth. The enthusiasm of the youth in National Socialist Germany is largely conditioned by the grandiose vision of a world united under German leadership and fascist domination. Democracy will be unable to defend itself against the fascist revolution if it remains only on the defensive and does not rise to the vision of a great revolution itself, if it will not act on the faith that this hour of its greatest dangers is also the hour of its greatest promise and highest adventure. Now is the time when it must realize its promise — to all classes and all races — of a fuller and richer life, based upon the liberty and dignity of every individual, upon the equality of all men, and upon the brotherhood of all peoples. At the beginning of the war in 1939 many people in the democracies began to realize the interdependence of all nations on this earth in the twentieth century. Many suggestions of a union now among the democracies, of a close federation of the United States with the English-speaking peoples of the British Commonwealth of Nations, of a world federation and a world government, pointed, full of challenge and promise, in the right direction. War in our time will have to bring about a closer union on this shrinking earth. The question which is being decided is whether this union will come by the sword of the conqueror, imposing upon the globe the hard rule of a master race and the unity of fascist discipline, or by the coöperation of free peoples shouldering courageously the burden which the conditions of the twentieth century place upon them.

COALESCE OR COLLIDE

Der eigentliche Unterscheidungsgrund liegt darin: ob man an ein absolut Erstes und Ursprüngliches im Menschen selber, an Freiheit, an unendliche Verbesserlichkeit, an ewiges Fortschreiten unseres Geschlechts glaube, oder ob man an alles dieses nicht glaube. . . . Alle . . . die, die Freiheit wenigstens ahnen, und sie nicht hassen oder vor ihr erschrecken, sondern sie lieben: alle diese sind ursprüngliche Menschen, sie sind, wenn sie als ein Volk betrachtet werden, ein Urvolk, das Volk schlechtweg, Deutsche. . . . Was an Geistigkeit und Freiheit dieser Geistigkeit glaubt, und die ewige Fortbildung dieser Geistigkeit durch Freiheit will, das, wo es auch geboren sey und in welcher Sprache es rede, ist unsers Geschlechts, es gehört uns an und es wird sich zu uns ˟hun. Was an Stillstand, Rückgang und Cirkeltanz glaubt, oder gar eine todte Natur an das Ruder der Weltregierung setzt, dieses, wo auch es geboren sey und welche Sprache es rede, ist undeutsch und fremd für uns, und es ist zu wünschen, dass es je eher je lieber sich gänzlich von uns abtrenne.

JOHANN GOTTLIEB FICHTE, Addresses to the German Nation. (*Sämmtliche Werke*, Leipzig, 1922, vol. VII, pp. 374, 375.)

[The real distinction is between those who believe in the creative spontaneity of man, in his freedom and unlimited perfectibility, in an unending progress of the human race, and those who do not believe in all that. . . . All men who do not hate or fear freedom of man, but love it, are . . . if regarded as one nation, members of *the* nation, are Germans. . . . Whoever believes in the freedom of the spirit and desires the eternal progress of spiritual life, he, whatever his birth or his language, belongs to us and will join us. Whoever denies progress or puts dead nature up as governing this world, he, whatever his birth or his language, is no German and is alien to us; he should completely separate himself from us as fast as possible.]

Coalesce or Collide

THE nineteenth century offers the apparent paradox of an unparalleled intensity of cultural intercourse between peoples — sometimes between those most widely separated geographically — and at the same time a completely novel bitterness in conflicts between nations. The development of science and of communication brought about not only a complete change in economic relationships but a growing approximation of all civilized life on the five continents to a similar pattern; a unified humanity with a common cultural design seemed to emerge at the beginning of the twentieth century; but at the same time the divisions within mankind became more pronounced than ever before, conflicts between them spread over wider areas, stirred deeper emotions. Cultural contact had engendered and intensified conflict between nationalities.

On the European continent political life in the modern sense of the word began with the French Revolution. This carried a great and generous message of new liberty and dignity to all individuals and to all peoples. Using propaganda and the force of arms it spread the universal message with missionary zeal; but it spread it as a French message establishing the superiority of French civilization as the most rational, enlightened, and humane type of civilization.

The new and deeper renaissance to which all Europe aspired in the eighteenth century was first realized in France. The eyes of Europe were turned toward the source from which the light came; it was contact with the ideas of the French Revolution which awakened the then dormant political life and thought in other European countries, especially in Germany and Italy. French nationalism set the example for the unification of a nation; in Italy and Germany French armies swept away most of the feudal encumbrances which impeded the process of national unification. But the combination of cosmopolitan individualism with French nationalism, which appeared natural to the French, could not be accepted by the non-French peoples who came under the influence of the French Revolution. Within twenty-five years the French Revolution transformed the intellectual and social life of Germany and Italy. The idea that a tyrant might be expelled, the cult of liberty, the aspiration toward nationhood one and indivisible, the longing for a new national cohesion and a new national spirit, the idea of a state rooted in popular consent and enthusiasm — all these concepts of the French Revolution spread to Italy and Germany, were eagerly learned from France. But the emphasis shifted; the tyrants to be expelled were French influence and French armies of occupation; the liberty worshipped was not so much individual freedom from authoritarian government as national freedom from foreign governments. The great Italian nationalist of this period, Vincenzo

Cuoco, summed up this shift in attitude in his *Saggio Storico* of the Neapolitan revolution of 1799. "Strange character of all the peoples of this earth!" he exclaimed. "The desire to give them an exaggerated liberty awakens in them a longing for freedom from the liberators themselves."

The new feeling of nationalism and of national pride spreading throughout Europe was, naturally, opposed to the French nationalism from which it had received its great impulse. Each new nationalism looked for its justification to its own national heritage and strove for its glorification. Fighting against the preponderant influence of French authors, each extolled the beauty of its own language and literature in contrast to that of the French. Out of the myths of the past and out of dreams of the future German and Italian authors created an ideal fatherland long before it became a political reality. The process of building a nation was reversed. In France, as in Great Britain and the United States, the struggle for a new political and social reality had preceded or at least accompanied the cultural rejuvenation of the nation; in Germany and Italy the cultural rejuvenation preceded, and was separated from, the political and social transformation. The nationalism of the French Revolution was indissolubly linked with individual liberty and rational cosmopolitanism. Nationalism in Germany and Italy, born under the influence of and in the struggle against France, necessarily tended for its own self-preservation and development to empha-

size elements diametrically contrary to the very essence of French nationalism. This nationalism thus
became not only anti-French, but a revolt against
rationalism and cosmopolitan tendencies. The contact between cultures not only generated and deepened a conflict between nations but produced a
cultural conflict which invested the struggle between
nations with the halo of a semi-religious crusade.

In the main the cultural intercourse followed the
line of the cultural gradient and moved from centers
of greater cultural intensity to those of lesser. In a
dialectic process of action and counteraction the
French Revolution, at once political and cultural,
rejuvenated Germany and Italy. Similarly German
literature in the time of Herder and of romanticism
rejuvenated the intellectual life of the western Slavs.
Herder had drawn a picture of the pacific and democratic Slavs as victims of feudal warrior nations like
the German. "They were charitable," he says of the
Slavs, "prodigally hospitable, lovers of rural freedom,
but subservient and obedient, enemies of robbing and
plundering. All that did not help them against oppression. On the contrary, it contributed to bring it about.
Thus several nations, especially the German, sinned
against them." He deplored the unhappiness of the
Slavs of his day and he foresaw for them a glorious
future of quiet industry, once they were awakened
from their long slumber and liberated from their
chains. And he insistently expressed the desire to see
them cultivate their own language and their tradi-

tional arts. Slavic students who came to German universities or read German books received from German sources the inspiration for their own nationalism, for their own efforts to revive the Slavic languages and civilization. They were filled with a new sense of the future greatness of the Slav race. This new conviction gave them a deep sense of obligation to liberate Slavic life from the cultural, and later on from the political, impact of Germany. By expanding Herder's characterization of the relationship between Slavs and Germans the great Czech historian, František Palacký, arrived at a construction of Czech history which could serve as a foundation for Czech nationalism and as a justification of Czech opposition to Germany's cultural and political domination. Over against the aggressive and conquering-warrior spirit of German feudal society he set the idyllic picture of the pacific and democratic Slav community. According to him its anti-authoritarian and liberty-loving spirit had asserted itself throughout Czech civilization, especially in the Hussite movement and in the Bohemian Brethren. In Bohemia had been sown the first seeds of liberalism and enlightenment which were later on carried to western Europe. The struggle of the Czechs against the Germans was therefore not only a conflict between national groups but a struggle between opposing ideals of civilization, the ideals of democracy and authoritarianism. Thomas Masaryk, in this respect a disciple of Palacký, built upon this concept his interpretation of history and applied it to contemporary politics. The cultural contact between Germans and Slavs had aroused Slavic nationalism. This in turn rebelled against Germanic influences and sought its justification in a reconstruction of the past that would oppose German with Slavic ideas.

When Thomas Macaulay in 1835 presented his Memorandum on education in India, contact between the civilizations of Europe and Asia had for centuries been slight and superficial. In this Memorandum he proposed to spread a knowledge of European literature and science amongst the Indians and to promote English education and English ideals for India. The reform following on the Memorandum created a new India and its effects were felt all over Asia. Through contact with England a generation of Indian intellectuals imbued with English ideas of freedom and self-government grew up. Under the impact of English ideas and in imitation of English political methods these intellectuals, with the help of English liberals, in 1885 created the Indian National Congress, the first representative organization of public opinion in Asiatic lands. The intellectual and moral stir in India, known as the Indian National Movement, was entirely a product of the cultural contact of India with Great Britain. The application of English ideas to Indian life awakened an Indian desire for nationhood, led to an agitation against the continuation of British domination over India. And soon Indian nationalism, a product of British influence, was bound to object not only to Britain's political domination but to her cultural influence. India's self-realization as a nation, in order to be Indian, had to be different from that of England. Indian nationalism, which had originally been an insistence upon the right to revolt and to demand constitutional liberties (in the wake of and as a product of English constitutional liberalism), was transformed into a moral obligation to protect national customs and the destiny of the country from foreign influence, and in particular from an imitation of English liberalism. Legends of the past and dreams of the future combined to create a vision of India's peculiar and unique task in the service of mankind. A mission was discovered for India: to set Indian spiritualism and metaphysical profundity over against Western materialism and physical (superficial) comfort. Indian religiosity was to save Europe from its permanent strife and chaos. And this goal was set before Indian youth, sometimes with extravagant exuberance:

> You shall help to create a nation, to spiritualize an epoch, to Aryanize the world. And that nation is your own, that epoch belongs to you and your children, and that world is no mere tract of land, but the whole earth with its teeming millions.

Many students have referred to the difference in the character of nationalism in Western Europe and elsewhere. This difference can be partly explained by the fact that the growth to nationhood in England and France was to a large extent a process of internal or immanent growth, a product of indigenous social and political forces, whereas nationalism in Central and Eastern Europe and in Asia began its development under outside influence. This so-to-speak derived nationalism, almost entirely a product of cultural contact, took two different forms, according to the specific reaction to the outside influence. The one accepted the Western form of nationalism with its implications and wished to apply it to the newly awakened nations. It sought in the political form developed by Western nationalism, in British parliamentary institutions and in the French republican tradition, a universally applicable model. The modern industrial order, which had developed simultaneously with modern nationalism in Western Europe, was welcomed and furthered as laying the social foundations for the desired form of nationhood. These nationalists, whom we may call Westerners or liberals, are clearly the product of cultural contact and know themselves as such. They are to be found in Germany as well as in Russia and in India. In Germany Kant, Friedrich Christoph Schlosser, Karl Rotteck, Georg Gottfried Gervinus, Georg Herwegh, to name only a few, represented this tendency, which found its home in southwestern Germany especially. In the left wing of the Frankfurt Parliament it had tried for the first time to shape a Germany according to the Western pattern. It was defeated in the spring of 1849. It was by no means dead then, but the hope of its renewed strength was cut short by Bismarck's successes and later on by the fact that in the tragic death of Emperor Frederick III the expectations of moderate liberalism were frustrated in Germany. William I was a representative of the *Vormärz*, William II a product of the Bismarckian empire. It was the tragedy of Germany and Europe that partly through historical accident, certainly not because of any innate trait in the German people, the generation of 1848 never had its day in Germany.

Stronger than this tendency toward Westernism in German nationalism — a tendency which was the direct result of cultural contact and knew itself as such — was the trait which emphasized German peculiarity and uniqueness and which set itself outside the influence of cultural contact with alien civilizations. It appealed to the differences in the historical past of Germany and Western Europe rather than to their common development, conditioned by the oneness of human reason. The French historian Michelet, in the spirit of 1848, had expressed the conviction that with the growth of culture man becomes more and more independent of the bonds of nature and the past:

In this marvellous transformation the spirit has triumphed over matter, the general over the particular and the idea over reality, the barbarian periods represent almost nothing but the local, the particular, the material. Man still clings to the soil, he seems to be part of it. . . . Slowly the strength which is the real essence of man will detach him, will uproot him from this soil. . . . He will need, instead of his native village, instead of his town or his province, a great fatherland.

The idea of this fatherland, an abstract idea which owes little to the senses, will carry him through a new effort to the idea of a universal fatherland, of the City of Providence.

German historiography, on the contrary, turned to the soil and to the indelible natural character of each people for guidance. No common road for humanity was acknowledged. Liberalism and popular sovereignty, individual rights and modern industrial society, were regarded as products of the West, unsuited to Germany. Germany had to find its own solution for its problems, and had to find it in its own past and its own character. Romantic historiography in Germany, which claimed to go back to the eternal principles and to the unchangeable nature of things, in reality often based its conclusions upon a hasty generalization from insufficient observation of contemporary events. It regarded the French Revolution as mere destructive chaos and the absolutism of Napoleon as characteristic of the persistent character of the French nation. Fichte, in his *Addresses to the German Nation*, defined German statecraft as an education of the individual for liberty, independence, originality; whereas the French, and the Romance peoples in general, according to Fichte, inclined to imitation, uniformity, dependence upon authority, and therefore to absolutism and one-man rule. Fichte himself was a liberal, a disciple of Kant and of the French Revolution, and in spite of many seeming aberrations he remained fundamentally faithful to the ideas of his youth. But he shared the dominant German tendency to construct an irreconcilable opposition between Germanism and the West — with the latter seen as the principle of superficiality, the former as that of depth. This romantic nationalism glorified the pre-capitalistic political and social order, the municipal guilds, the patrimonial rule of an agrarian nobility, the immobility of the Berufstände. Liberalism and democracy were looked upon as products of alien principles, conducive to revolution and chaos.

It should, however, be pointed out that some of the German Westernizers and liberals also discovered in the German past the basis for their convictions. Gervinus in his introduction to the *History of the Nineteenth Century* declared democracy and federalism products of the Germanic and Protestant spirit. He fully accepted the glorious principles of 1789, but for him they represented the victory of the Germanic striving for individual liberty as over against the uniformity of Rome.

German romantic nationalism, produced by contact with Western modes of thought, bitterly conscious of Germany's inferiority as compared with the West and therefore flaunting its own alleged superiority defiantly and triumphantly, had its counterpart in Russian Slavophilism. Its origin and attitudes corresponded with those of German romantic nationalism; but Germany was included in the West which was rejected. Slavophilism opposed the Westernization of Russia, and saw in Peter the Great a destructive force which had turned Russia away from the strength that springs from a purely indigenous development and had instead opened her up to cultural contact with the West. The Slavophiles rejected liberalism, individualism, and modern economic development. They believed the salvation of Russia to lie in strict adherence to its medieval foundations, its orthodox religious life, its autocratic form of government, and its traditional agrarian economy. The Slavophiles regarded the Russian as an *Urvolk*, just as Fichte had regarded the Germans. They exalted the role Russia was to play in the salvation of mankind, and especially in that of the decaying West. Magnicky, governmental censor under Alexander I, saw in the Tartar yoke perhaps the greatest blessing of Russian history, for it had kept Russia isolated from Europe and had thus preserved her purity. Russia, which through her strength and faith had liberated Europe from the scourge of Napoleon and the Revolution, needed no cultural contacts with Europe; rather, Europe needed to learn from Russia. Shishkov, Minister of Education, thought capital punishment fitting for anyone who would propose to introduce the Latin script into Russia.

But Slavophilism was opposed in Russia by a long line of Westernizers and reformers — from the Decembrists in 1825 to the liberals in the provisional government of 1917. These saw the salvation of Russia as lying in acceptance of Western ideologies, and Western economic progress and political constitutions — in Russia's adaptation to and participation in the general course of mankind's development. In many ways, and in a rather unexpected form, Leninism led the Westernizing tendencies in Russia to their triumph. Hitlerism on the other hand marked the triumph of a vulgarized exaggeration of romantic nationalism in Germany. Both were adaptations to the imperatives of an age of mass movements.

The reaction to cultural contact, as represented by German romantic nationalism and by Slavophilism, is not a development confined to Germany and Russia. It is found in every part of the earth where national consciousness has been aroused by cultural contact with the West. The liberal Westernizers and social reformers in India found themselves opposed by the new nationalism of a Tilak and a Gandhi, for whom the very fact that the Indian people have remained so "uncivilized" is a thing of merit. In the first place Gandhi did not repudiate British political domination; he rejected European civilization. "One effort is required," he said, "and that is to drive out Western civilization. All else will follow." Western civilization seemed to him primarily economic and therefore materialistic. India's salvation lay for him in the revival of traditional Indian forms of life. The renaissance of the spinning wheel became the center of Gandhi's hopes. But Gandhi is mistaken when he thinks of his nationalism as an indigenous Indian growth. It would have been unthinkable without the cultural contact with the West; it is not a return to

pre-British days; it is very definitely a phenomenon
arising out of an acquaintance with certain elements
of European civilization — with Ruskin, with Tolstoy,
with the European voices raised in protest against the
materialism of Western civilization, with the redis-
covery and reappraisal of India's past by European
scholars.

In the same way German or Russian romantic nationalism, which deepened political and economic
competition among the states of the world by intro-
ducing an ideological conflict touching upon the
ultimate destiny of nations and mankind, was in no
way a product of indigenous development, of a unique
and exclusive originality, of *Eigenart* and *samobyt-
nost*: it was a product of cultural contact and of an
erroneous interpretation of the past. Most of the
political ideas of the German romanticists came from
the West, from Burke, de Maistre, and Bonald. The
love for the simple, common people was derived from
Rousseau. The racial theory of Richard Wagner and
Houston Stewart Chamberlain, to whom Hitler is so
much indebted, was inspired by Count Gobineau.
The anti-parliamentarian vehemence of the German
and Italian nationalists of the right, their predilection
for the sword as arbiter, and their anti-economic insistence upon the precedence of political considerations (especially those of foreign policy) over social
and economic problems were anticipated by Charles
Maurras. Even the famous slogan *Blut und Boden*
was foreshadowed in Maurice Barrès' *la terre et les*

morts. Barrès, speaking of *"l'acceptation des nécessités de la vie"* and insisting that "the human plant grows vigorously only so long as it remains subject to the conditions which shaped and preserved its species during the centuries," was followed by Hitler — who builds his system upon what he calls the iron logic of nature, and winds up in a complete biological determinism.

There had been the same dependence of Germany on the West in the past. From its very inception German civilization was molded by its contacts with other ways of life, and it grew through a process of continuous cultural contact with other ways of life. This is especially true of the German civilization of the Middle Ages, upon whose national and original character romanticism liked to speculate. Nor was Russian Slavophilism any more unique. In fact it owes most of its ideas to the influence of German romanticism. Even its love for the mujik is only an echo of the myth of the noble savage. Its economic leitmotif, the glorification of the Russian agrarian community, the *mir*, received its directing impetus from a conservative German student of rural conditions, August von Haxthausen, who saw in the *mir*, as did the Slavophiles, an organic development out of the depths of the Russian folk-soul. Later on it was demonstrated that such village communities were in no way confined to the Russians or the Slavs, and that the Russian *mir*, far from being in its present form an early indigenous institution or an expression of basic national ideals, had developed in fairly recent times — either as a governmental measure to facilitate tax collecting or as the result of social and economic forces growing out of the increasing pressure of population.

In modern times the forms taken all over the world by national reactions to cultural contact can be reduced to rather uniform patterns. At one extreme stands the negative pattern, represented by the resistance of the Chinese imperial government to the Westernization of China. This resistance took the form of a complete refusal to allow any intercourse between China and the rest of the world. It was an almost totalitarian isolationism; a rejection of the concept of the family of nations and the coöperation of equal states. This complete isolationism led to a number of conflicts in which the Chinese Empire was the loser. That China did not perish entirely in the process may be attributed, on the one hand, less to its vast area and the size of its population than (as Professor MacNair rightly points out) to the failure of the imperialist nations to agree upon a division of the spoils; and on the other hand to the generally enlightened though not unselfish policies of the trader-empires, Great Britain and the United States. At the other extreme stands the Turkish Republic under the leadership of Mustapha Kemal. Contemporary Turkey eagerly sought and encouraged intercourse with the West. The result was not only a complete Europeanization of all the external forms of life but an acceptance of the basic attitudes underlying the achievements of the

West. The past was completely discarded, traditional ties were cut. Without reservation Turkey entered the modern age. The ideological base of the present government — economic reconstruction, democratic equality of rights, international peace and tolerance — implies a full acquiescence in the rational and progressive liberalism of the nineteenth century, which is Europe's legacy from the French Revolution. In spite of its transitional dictatorship, Turkey belongs fundamentally with the democracies. During the nineteenth century Westernism and Orientalism fought a protracted duel in Turkey; in the last twenty years Westernism has definitely gained the upper hand, to the exclusion of all isolationist and romantic elements. So far as we can judge at present, Turkey has drawn new strength from her complete transformation and has entirely changed her status in the family of nations.

Between these two extremes, China and Turkey, we may place the more complex phenomena of contemporary Prussia and Japan. They provide the two most important examples of a voluntary adoption of certain aspects of cultural contact — of an intercourse that has been strictly selective and consciously guided in order to gain new strength for national conflicts. With methodical skill Prussia after 1806, Japan after 1871, adopted (and with a high degree of success) the modern forms of social life and administration whose seeds were germinated by the French Revolution and by industrial civilization. Both countries had resisted until events convinced them that without thorough-going internal reforms they would be unable to maintain their position and independence. The speed, energy, and purposefulness with which the task was carried out in the two nations was remarkable and admirable. But the reforms were undertaken with no thought of changing the core of Prussian and Japanese tradition to bring them in line with the philosophy of the French Revolution and of an industrial society. They were instituted to give a surer protection to traditional habits of thought and to the social and moral values of the past. Cultural contact brought an outward adjustment in national life, but this was accompanied by a hardening of the core under the new protective armor. The maladjustments ensuing from the discrepancy between outward form and inner life have proved in the last few decades to be the most disturbing factor in international relations and one of the deepest sources of the present strife between nations.

Cultural contact in the sense discussed here is, of course, a phenomenon as old as history. But only in the last century has this cultural intercourse become world-wide, drawing all peoples into its orbit and reaching down to the masses in an effort to revolutionize their traditional life. The logical outcome of this process would be the development of a world order and a world civilization. But the irrational forces of history, the vested emotional and social interests surviving from the past, have revolted against this trend. The present great conflict of nations, which has raged now for several years on the battlefields of three continents and has been evident in the moral and mental confusion in all countries, has many different causes. Many purely local factors have contributed to its outbreak and growth. But, if we dare subsume all its different aspects under one general cause, we may regard the conflict as the outcome of the historical process of cultural contact on a worldwide scale. Assuming many masks and seizing upon various pretexts, it is the struggle between the two opposed patterns of reacting to the meeting of cultures — the rational and liberal pattern of coöperation, and the irrational pattern which, spellbound by the past, stresses isolationism and peculiarities above the growing oneness and common destiny of contemporary mankind.

EDUCATION FOR THE COMING ERA

Considerate la vostra semenza:
Fatti non foste a viver come bruti,
Ma per seguir virtute e conoscenza.

DANTE, *Inferno*, XXVI, 118–120.

. . . Come my friends,
'Tis not too late to seek a newer world.
Push off, and sitting well in order smite
The sounding furrows; for our purpose holds
To sail beyond the sunset, and the baths
Of all the western stars until we die.
It may be that the gulf will wash us down,
It may be we shall touch the happy isles
And see the great Achilles whom we knew.
Though much is taken, much abides and though
We are not now that strength which in old days
Moved earth and heaven: that which we are, we are: —
One equal temper of heroic hearts
Made weak by time and fate, but strong in will
To strive, to seek, to find, and not to yield.

TENNYSON, *Ulysses*.

Education for the Coming Era

TWO thousand years and more ago, in a situation strikingly similar to the one in which we find ourselves today, a man of Greece, who saw more clearly and spoke more courageously than most of his contemporaries, uttered warnings against a military autocracy that threatened his country from without. His warnings were unheeded because they were unwelcome. That man was Demosthenes, the Athenian orator, who lived in a period when the citizens of Athens — leading democracy of the Greek city-states — seemingly secure in their prosperity and isolation, were oblivious to impending dangers. Perhaps they thought that the day of world empires was gone forever, whereas in reality the greatest of those empires were still to come. Athens was full of false prophets who circulated among the people, offering advice that rings familiarly in our ears today: "Athenians, mind your own business. Preserve your own peace. Let other peoples take care of themselves, work out their own problems, fight their own battles."

I wish to set before you here for your consideration half a dozen passages from various speeches of Demosthenes, delivered in the fourth century before our era. Change the names of places and of persons, and these same words might have been said in England or in France two years ago. With equal force they could, and should, have been said in the United States at least twelve months ago.

Read this:

Men of Athens, I want you to know and realize two things: first, what an expensive game it is to squander your interests one by one: and secondly, the restless activity which is ingrained in Philip's nature, and which makes it impossible for him ever to rest on his laurels.[1]

And this:

Seriously, is anyone here so foolish as not to see that our negligence will transfer the war from Chalcidice to Attica? Yet if that comes to pass, I am afraid, men of Athens, that just as men who borrow money recklessly at high interest enjoy a temporary accommodation only to forfeit their estates in the end, so we may find that we have paid a heavy price for our indolence, and because we consult our own pleasure in everything, may hereafter come to be forced to do many of the difficult things for which we had no liking, and may finally endanger our possessions here in Attica itself.[2]

And then this:

The chief object, however, of his arms and his diplomacy is our free constitution: on nothing in the world is he more bent than on its destruction. And it is in a way natural that he should act thus. For he knows for certain that even if he masters all else, his power will be precarious as long as you remain a democracy; but if ever he meets with one of the many mischances to which mankind is liable, all the forces that are now under restraint will be attracted to your side.[3]

[1] Demosthenes, with an English Translation by J. H. Vince. (The Loeb Classical Library), p. 13.
[2] *Ibid.*, p. 13.   [3] *Ibid.*, pp. 197, 199.

And this:

But if anyone mistakes for peace an arrangement which will enable Philip, when he has seized everything else, to march upon us, he has taken leave of his senses, and the peace that he talks of is one that you observe towards Philip, but not Philip towards you.[4]

And this:

Men of Athens, you have deserted the post in which your ancestors left you; you have been persuaded by politicians . . . that to be paramount in Greece, to possess a standing force, and to help all the oppressed, is a superfluous task and an idle expense; while you fondly imagined that to live in peace, to neglect all your duties, to abandon all your possessions and let others seize them one by one, ensured wonderful prosperity and complete security.[5]

Finally, consider this passage from the speech "For the Liberty of the Rhodians," in which Demosthenes pleads with the Athenians to come to the aid of the Rhodian democrats and help them to resist the aggression of Philip and his fellow oligarchs:

Seeing that Chios and Mytilene are ruled by oligarchs, and that Rhodes and, I might almost say, all the world are now being seduced into this form of slavery, I am surprised that none of you conceives that our constitution too is in danger, nor draws the conclusion that if all other states are organized on oligarchical principles, it is impossible that they should leave your democracy alone. For they know that none but you will bring freedom back again, and of course they want to destroy the source from which they are expecting ruin to themselves.[6]

[4] *Ibid.*, p. 229.   [5] *Ibid.*, p. 295.   [6] *Ibid.*, p. 423.

What was the situation in Greece when Demosthenes was thus exhorting the Athenians to rouse themselves to the truth of their position and resist the impending peril to their democracy? At that time, the country was divided into small city-states, each isolationist in its political philosophy, each supposedly secure in its own strength against all the world. To the suggestion that these separate city-states might perish before the new techniques of aggression which were being developed by the great powers that moved beyond their borders, the Greeks willfully shut their minds. Fighting planes and dive bombers were still things of the distant future; nevertheless, the Macedonians were then perfecting methods of attack hitherto untried, and the question that the Greeks were forced to face was whether they should cling to the individual sovereignty and isolation of their cities or unify themselves for mutual assistance and protection.

History tells us what their answer was. They refused to join together, and ultimately they succumbed, all of them one by one, to Philip. Greek liberty was gone. Greek democracy had perished. Athens was no longer a city of free men; it had ceased to be the light for all mankind.

II

I have said that the situation of the Greeks in the days when Philip threatened and Demosthenes warned was similar to our own today. I wish now to point out two important differences that we should never overlook. The first difference is that Greece was only a small part of the world. Beyond its limits lay whole continents, still unknown. In these lands there might be born — as there has been — a sort of liberty then undreamed of. Today, there are no undiscovered continents, no frontiers still waiting to be opened up. The whole world has become one, and its destiny is one. In the place of Greece as it was then stand today all the democracies and all hope for future freedom.

The second and more important difference between the fate that overtook the Greeks and the possibility that confronts us now lies in the nature of the threatening force. Alexander the Great, who realized, or tried to realize, the ambitions of his father, Philip, was not antagonistic to Athenian civilization. On the contrary, being a disciple of Aristotle, Alexander had come to venerate the culture of the Greeks; he felt himself to be a Hellene. More than that, he considered himself the instrument by which that culture was to be disseminated far beyond the country of its origin. In reality, as all students of history know, it was Alexander who pointed the way to the birth of Stoic philosophy, with its recognition of the universal brotherhood of men in a rational world, and so made possible the greatest flowering of ancient civilization.

The forces that threaten the democracies today are openly hostile to the democratic spirit; they do not look upon themselves as heirs or carriers of the traditions of western civilization. They are doing what

Alexander never did; they are leading a revolution against our civilization; a determined and conscious attack upon all that is basic to it. If they are victorious, the form and spirit of our life — our social life, our personal life — will be changed. Everything that we call good will be called evil, and everything that we call evil will be called good.

If, now, we ask ourselves what is the real root of the present trouble that afflicts our world, we have to go back twenty years and reëxamine the Treaty of Versailles. Without rehearsing the details, we can say that we had an opportunity, by means of the great promises contained in this peace treaty, to do the three things that would have given us a firm basis for building a new world. If the ideals of Woodrow Wilson had been realized and if the spirit of enlightened liberalism had prevailed, these three things for which the foundations were well laid in the Treaty of Versailles might have been accomplished.

The first was to break Prussian militarism, that incubus upon the German people which was a menace to all of Europe; the second was to liberate oppressed peoples and to give them a new sense of dignity and happiness; and the third was to form an association of the free peoples throughout the world for common protection — the League of Nations.

The tragedy is that none of these three goals of the Treaty of Versailles was attained. None of them was fulfilled, not because of the "wickedness" of the governments, but because of the unwillingness of the peoples of the world to shoulder the burden of the peace treaties. In their shortsightedness they believed that they were still living in the nineteenth century. They did not realize that in 1919 a period of history had come to an end and a new era had begun. When the war was over they relapsed into their old habits of thought, shrank back into isolation, and allowed themselves once more to be dominated by intense feelings of alleged self-interest and of nationalism.

In the United States, the decade of the nineteen-twenties was one of disillusionment, of "debunking" as it was called. It was also a period of wishful thinking during which the American people persuaded themselves that they had at last achieved complete security, and that no new forces would ever again upset the established scheme of things. They refused to see that, as the Greek city-state had outlived its effectiveness in the fourth century B.C., just so the isolated and sovereign state of modern times, which developed between the Renaissance and the years of the first world war, had lost the basis for its existence in a new world of rapid communication. Instead of recognizing this change and addressing themselves to the task of creating a new world for a new mankind, they persistently turned aside from any deeper understanding of the new forces, from any firm moral choice that would have involved the assuming of personal responsibility.

III

In this hour of crisis, we are face to face with the question that confronted the Greeks in the time of Philip — the question of choosing between isolation and unity. If, like the Greeks, we allow the decision on this vital issue to go by default, we risk not only the loss of our liberties, as they did, but the far greater disaster of the destruction of the spiritual, moral, and intellectual values which we and our forebears have cherished and for which our fathers fought.

During the post-war period, and even in the midst of the preparations for a new and infinitely more decisive war, we have chosen isolation. By "we" I do not mean only the people of the United States, although they were the first to slip back into isolation in 1919 and have been the last to awaken from its comfort. I mean the peoples of all the democracies, and in each democracy I mean the people as a whole. Isolationism was not the fault of any one class, as, for instance, the British Tories. It has been characteristic of all classes during the last twenty fateful years; many socialists indeed out-chamberlained Chamberlain. The task of trying to unite the peoples of the world has been blindly left by the democracies to the dictators. And the dictators are attempting to achieve this task, not by reason, but by brute force and the degradation of man; they are not working in the interests of human freedom and dignity, but are seeking everywhere to overthrow them.

How effectively have we educators come to the defense of reason and freedom? How fully are we living in this new world? Are not most of us still dwelling in an imaginary prewar world, fascinated and paralyzed, unable to comprehend the forces that are changing reality far beyond any parallel with 1914? What have we done through education to concentrate the mind of the rising generation upon the one essential problem of the twentieth century, upon a true understanding of history and its forces? Have we not rather filled the minds of our people with so great a diversity of things that they have been distracted from the effort to concentrate upon the essential? Have we not increased their sentimentalism and their belief that wishful thinking, through the intensity of its sincerity alone, will blossom forth into reality? Have we not failed to show them that in the long run no democracy or decent life at home is possible, under twentieth-century conditions, if it is not first and above all internationally secure? Have we in any way helped our people to realize that whatever happens anywhere on earth happens to them?

The consequence of our attitude was that in the fateful months of the summer of 1939 we had no true understanding of the situation which we were facing. The success of fascism during the fourth decade of the twentieth century was due to its profound recognition of the fact that the struggle to come was not to be about frontiers or about raw materials, about markets or about migrations, but was to decide the future of civilization everywhere. The world was to be united. The question remained whether the unification was to take place under the leadership of the liberal and democratic forces that had come to the fore as the result of the Anglo-Saxon and French revolutions of the seventeenth and eighteenth centuries, or was to be imposed by the great counter-revolution represented by European fascism and Japanese militarism. The democratic peoples refused to shoulder the burden that the twentieth century put upon them; they are now paying the price for this refusal.

We were in no way prepared for the inevitable conflict. In September 1939 we and the smaller democracies in Europe believed that we could escape the struggle by simply ignoring its existence. We tried to hide ourselves behind a wall of cynicism, behind denial that moral values were at stake, behind the complacent hope that if we minded our own business somehow the conflagration would not spread and reach our shores. Everywhere those who had criticized Chamberlain now outdid him; and to justify their "neutrality" they found fault with the attacked and made excuses for the aggressors. Thus it happened that in the hour of supreme test, when the democracies were faced with the immense responsibility of deciding the future for themselves and for civilization, they were totally unprepared to meet the test.

The danger to democracy arose out of failure to comprehend the issues that were involved. The final realization of their danger shocked the democracies into action, sometimes when it was very late, always when it was later than they thought; but it did not in every case arouse them to a full awareness of the truth that a world revolution is now in progress.

It is imperative that without further delay we concentrate all our intellectual and moral resources upon the one task of freeing our people from the lack of understanding, from the illusions and fears, that shackle them and make them undecided, hesitating, and panic-stricken instead of resolute and farsighted. We must help them to see clearly what they wish to do and thus to gain the strength that springs from understanding knowledge and from devotion to a common and constructive purpose. We must equip them to live and function in the world of the twentieth century, which will be, whether we wish it or not, a unified world under a common leadership. Our responsibility is to see that in this new world the dignity and worth of the individual shall be respected, the equality of men and races shall be recognized, the freedom of all shall be safeguarded; in short, that it shall be a world in which democracy will grow and peace will be assured. Such a world cannot come in any easy way, not by soft living nor by minding our business; it can come only through a hard struggle, through many sacrifices, and through unflinching courage and devotion. Only thus can the great heritage of western civilization that springs from Athens and Jerusalem be preserved and transmitted to future generations, enriched and purified by the thought and toil, by the suffering and striving, of our generation.

. . . Adieu, monsieur; je vous recommande la vérité, la liberté, et la vertu, trois seules choses pour lesquelles on doive aimer la vie.

VOLTAIRE, *Questions sur les miracles,*
XIe Lettre

A LIST OF BOOKS

A List of Books

THE following bibliography confines itself to a few recent books which may help the reader to elucidate the problems connected with war in our time. With very few exceptions, only books published in 1939 and 1940 are included. This bibliography thus represents a continuation of that given in *Revolutions and Dictatorships*. For brief, expert, and most reliable accounts of current international topics the reader is referred to that excellent series, Oxford Pamphlets on World Affairs (Oxford University Press, Toronto, and Farrar and Rinehart, New York). *Foreign Affairs*, an American quarterly, publishes regularly valuable bibliographies of current books on international affairs and politics.

NORMAN ANGELL, *Why Freedom Matters* (London: Penguin Books, 1940).
A revindication of liberty as a necessary condition for waging and winning the present war.

RUTH NANDA ANSHEN (ed.), *Freedom: Its Meaning* (New York: Harcourt Brace, 1940).
A collection of forty-one essays, by distinguished contributors, on the meaning of freedom.

ALBERT CARR, *Juggernaut: The Path of Dictatorship* (New York: Viking, 1939).
A popular treatise on authoritarian government from Richelieu to Hitler.

ALFRED COBBAN, *Dictatorship: Its History and Theory* (New York: Scribner, 1939).
A scholarly and highly readable history of dictatorship from traditional monarchy to the modern totalitarian state.

GUY STANTON FORD (ed.), *Dictatorship in the Modern World* (second edition, University of Minnesota Press, 1939).

This second edition of a symposium which first appeared in 1935 discusses from the sociological and historical point of view the forms and aspects of dictatorship in Europe, in Latin America, and in the Far East.

GEORGE CATLIN, *Anglo-Saxony and Its Tradition* (New York: Macmillan, 1939).

A brilliant discussion of the Anglo-Saxon heritage and of the obligation which this heritage imposes on our time. "The issue will be between the discipline of a determined liberty and the discipline of despotism."

SIDNEY HOOK, *Reason, Social Myths, and Democracy* (New York: John Day, 1940).

A number of essays on leading social thinkers of the nineteenth and twentieth centuries.

R. M. MACIVER, *Leviathan and the People* (Louisiana State University Press, 1939).

A very well-written comparison of the genius of dictatorship and the genius of democracy.

ARCHIBALD MACLEISH, *The Irresponsibles: A Declaration* (New York: Duell, Sloan & Pearce, 1940).

One of the leading American intellectuals of our time discusses the responsibility of intellectuals in our time.

THOMAS MANN, *This War* (New York: Knopf, 1940).

An analysis of the fundamental spiritual causes of the second World War.

LEWIS MUMFORD, *Faith for Living* (New York: Harcourt, Brace & Co., 1940).

A forceful and moving appeal for a better understanding of our time. "We have a job to do, the hardest that ever faced a generation; harder still because it was sprung suddenly on us, and we have scarcely time to get our bearings before we plunge into it. Our job is to restore our own faith for living." A courageous challenge to the moral disintegration of our time.

RALPH BARTON PERRY, *Shall Not Perish from the Earth*
(New York: Vanguard Press, 1940).

The Harvard professor of philosophy discusses in this book, after
having summarized the democratic creed and the genius of America
on the one hand, and the philosophical roots of totalitarianism on
the other, the needs of the present hour, as regards limits of tolerance in domestic affairs and strength in foreign affairs as a condition
of survival.

MELVIN RADER, *No Compromise: The Conflict between Two
Worlds* (New York: Macmillan, 1939).

An American professor of philosophy takes up Mussolini's statement that "the struggle between two worlds can permit no compromise" from the democratic point of view.

ARNOLD J. TOYNBEE, *A Study of History*, vols. IV–VI
(New York: Oxford University Press, 1939).

A synthesis of history based upon a Christian and cosmopolitan
foundation. Of democracy the author says, "Its essence is a spirit
of fraternity which knows no bounds but those of life itself. The
natural field of action for democracy is then a field that embraces
all mankind; and it is on this range that its spiritual potency is
beneficent. But when this potent spiritual driving force is diverted
into the mechanism of a parochial state, it not only ceases to be
beneficent, but becomes malignant and subversive. Democracy
imprisoned in parochial states degenerates into nationalism." See
the review in *The Nation*, Feb. 7, 1940.

LEONARD WOOLF, *The War for Peace* (London: Routledge,
1940).

The longest and most interesting chapter of this book is a valuable
discussion of the often misunderstood interrelation of power, interests, and politics.

SIR ALFRED ZIMMERN, *Spiritual Values and World Affairs*
(Oxford: Clarendon Press, 1939).

These lectures were delivered in February, 1939, to students of
theology in Oxford. They deal with the fundamental questions
involved in a theological and philosophical appreciation of the
world situation between the two World Wars.

* * *

EDUARD BENEŠ, *Democracy Today and Tomorrow* (New York: Macmillan, 1939).

A sober and extremely well-balanced appreciation of democracy and the causes of its crisis. "As the very essence of the doctrine of fascism lies in the ability to accommodate itself at every moment to the momentary circumstances, without abandoning ever the final and permanent end of the whole doctrine, one must look at these formulas as momentary and the most dangerous opportunism."

EDWARD B. HITCHCOCK, *I Built a Temple for Peace: The Life of Eduard Beneš* (New York: Harper, 1940).

The biography of one of the foremost democrats of our time. Of great importance also is the latest authoritative biography of Beneš' teacher: Paul Selver, *Masaryk* (London: Michael Joseph, 1940).

WILLIAM E. RAPPARD, *The Quest for Peace* (Cambridge: Harvard University Press, 1940).

A detailed, scholarly, and extremely fair treatise on the problems of peace from the first World War to the outbreak of the second. The general reader will do well to read at least pages 470–501.

WALTER MILLIS, *Why Europe Fights* (New York: William Morrow, 1940).

A dispassionate story which nevertheless points out the guilt of those "who could never quite bring themselves to believe that Hitler and his associates really meant what they said, and who shrank from the risk of war and the cost of heavy rearmament," and who felt "that if they were careful not to annoy him, Hitler would come to a reasonable policy." See the review in *The Nation*, July 6, 1940.

DOROTHY THOMPSON, *Let the Record Speak* (Boston: Houghton Mifflin, 1939).

A noteworthy achievement by an American journalist who on the whole foresaw, as Churchill did, the true motives behind the earlier moves of National Socialist Germany.

EDMOND TAYLOR, *The Strategy of Terror* (Boston: Houghton Mifflin, 1940).

An indispensable account of German psychological war strategy by an American journalist who lived in France from 1933 to the end of 1939. "The great difference between the 1914 and the 1940 versions of war propaganda is that the former prostituted the hatred of evil to produce raw hate, whereas the latter prostitutes the love of peace, to produce sheer defeatism or even cowardice." "Let us intervene or not intervene, but above all let us not pretend to ourselves that the affair does not concern us; let us not prostitute the facts to justify our indifference. Because our indifference is not real and not natural; it is a hangover from the moral narcotics with which foreign and domestic propagandists have been doping us."

WINSTON CHURCHILL, *Step by Step, 1936–1939* (New York: Putnam, 1939).
The author reveals himself in this collection of parliamentary speeches as one of the few far-sighted statesmen of our time.

DUFF COOPER, *The Second World War* (London: Jonathan Cape, 1939).
Deals with the background of the present war up to the British declaration of war.

SIR NEVILE HENDERSON, *Failure of a Mission* (New York: Putnam, 1940).
This book gives us an insight into the mental attitudes of those wide circles in the democracies who were in definite sympathy with German aspirations and believed that National Socialism was out only to "right the wrongs of Versailles." See the review in *The Nation*, April 20, 1940.

VISCOUNT HALIFAX, *Speeches on Foreign Policy* (London: Oxford University Press, 1940).
This book is as characteristic as Sir Nevile Henderson's for the mental attitude of the liberal, well-meaning average mind which viewed events without the slightest comprehension of their true nature, and tried to be "reasonable" and business-like in face of a movement which scorned on principle any concessions or reasonable measures.

JOHN F. KENNEDY, *Why England Slept* (New York: Wilfred Funk, 1940).
The author, a young American who has lived in England in recent years, sees the reasons for England's plight in the fact that the English did not really believe that they would have to fight if they wished to maintain their freedom.

RAYMOND GRAM SWING, *How War Came* (New York: Norton, 1939).

Presents in book form the running commentary of a leading American radio commentator, from the seizure of Czecho-Slovakia to the invasion of Poland.

HELEN P. KIRKPATRICK, *Under the British Umbrella* (New York: Scribner, 1939).

Critical observations by an American journalist in Great Britain prior to the outbreak of the second World War.

ARTHUR GREENWOOD, *Why We Fight: Labour's Case* (London: Routledge, 1940).

One of the leaders of the British Labor party defines the point of view of the British Labor party in the present war.

HUGH DALTON, *Hitler's War: Before and After* (London: Penguin Books, 1940).

A discussion in some detail of the background of the present war and of the peace aims, by one of the leading members of the British Labor party.

WICKHAM STEED, *Our War Aims* (London: Secker & Warburg, 1939).

The well-known English journalist, who has a most intimate knowledge of Germany and Central Europe, defines the British attitude in this war.

HAROLD NICOLSON, *Why Britain Is at War* (London: Penguin Books, 1939).

A brilliant exposé of the motives which brought the British people reluctantly into the war.

NORMAN ANGELL, *For What Do We Fight?* (New York: Harper, 1939).

The author restates his views on peace and international organization which he has put forward since 1910, when he wrote *The Great Illusion*. He may be rightly regarded as the educator of a whole generation for the understanding of the fundamental issues confronting our time in the field of international politics.

C. E. M. JOAD, *Journey through the War Mind* (London: Faber, 1940).

The author is one of the leading absolute pacifists in England.

HESSELL TILTMAN, *Nightmares Must End* (London: Jarrolds, 1940).

The author sees the war in the Far East, in Spain, and in Europe as part of one great struggle.

J. ALVAREZ DEL VAYO, *Freedom's Battle* (New York: Knopf, 1940).

The history of the Spanish Civil War, told by the Foreign Minister and Minister of War in the republican government. A book of greatest significance.

ALBERT VITON, *Great Britain: An Empire in Transition* (New York: John Day, 1940).

"England has always lived dangerously, and it is difficult to see that she has been the worse for it. Rapid industrialization at the expense of agriculture was dangerous; very much so. . . . She ran tremendous risks when free trade was embraced, and again when it was abandoned . . . ; Lord Durham's recommendations, although inevitable, were dangerous, and the recent reforms in India and the colonies even more so. . . ."

M. PHILIPS PRICE, *Hitler's War in Eastern Europe* (London: Allen & Unwin, 1940).

An expert discussion of the problems of Eastern Europe in connection with the present war.

CARL J. HAMBRO, *I Saw It Happen in Norway* (New York: Appleton-Century, 1940).

A warning from Norway by the president of Norway's Parliament.

D. W. BROGAN, *France under the Republic* (New York: Harper, 1940).

This admirable and detailed history of the development of modern France from 1870 to 1939 does more for an understanding of the collapse of France than any of the many books now appearing and accounting for the downfall of the Third Republic. One of the first of these books to appear was André Maurois' *Tragedy in France: An Eye-Witness Account* (New York: Harper, 1940).

HEINZ POL, *Suicide of a Democracy* (New York: Reynal & Hitchcock, 1940).

So far probably the best of the books which try to explain the downfall of the French republic. A careful and balanced analysis. Less restrained in its criticism is André Simone, *J'Accuse! The Men*

Who Betrayed France (New York: The Dial Press, 1940). A careful and substantiated report of the events immediately preceding the surrender of France is offered by Hamilton Fish Armstrong, *Chronology of Failure: The Last Days of the French Republic* (New York: Macmillan, 1940).

* * *

HERMANN RAUSCHNING, *The Voice of Destruction (Hitler Speaks)* (New York: Putnam, 1940).

Probably one of the most revealing and important books about the aims and mentality of Chancellor Hitler. The author reports a number of conversations which he, as a member of the National Socialist Party, had with his leader in the years 1932–1934.

THORSTEIN VEBLEN, *Imperial Germany and the Industrial Revolution* (New York: Viking, 1939).

Reprint of a book which was first published in 1915. See the review by Henry A. Wallace in the *Political Science Quarterly*, September, 1940.

EDMOND VERMEIL, *L'Allemagne: Essai d'Explication* (Paris: Gallimard, 1940).

A very important and substantial book by the professor of German civilization at the Sorbonne, which bases an explanation of the Third Reich and of the present war upon an analysis of the social and intellectual history of Germany from the Holy Roman Empire on.

R. HINTON THOMAS, *German Perspectives* (Cambridge, England: Heffer, 1940).

A brief and somewhat compressed discussion of the literary tendencies of Germany in the period between the two wars. The attitude of German literature is important for the understanding of the political events in Germany. A larger book in this field is Jethro Bithell's *Modern German Literature, 1880–1938* (London: Methuen, 1939).

PETER F. DRUCKER, *The End of Economic Man* (New York: John Day, 1939).

A study of the heroic conception of life in the new totalitarian philosophy.

JAMES T. SHOTWELL, *What Germany Forgot* (New York: Macmillan, 1940).

An important analysis of the period between the two wars, by a leading American authority on history and international relations.

"Wholesale denunciation of the peace settlement of 1919 has served a political purpose which is the very opposite of what American liberals have set forth as their ideal. . . . The Treaty not only supplied a slogan of attack for the future, but dominated — and distorted — the perspective of history as well." "There lay behind the German action a history and a trend of thinking which accepted war as the instrument of the nation's policy, and therefore justified its costs and sacrifices as a normal process of . . . political evolution. . . . It was at this point that the Treaty of Versailles became, by an almost miraculous paradox, the instrument for saving German militarism."

OTTO D. TOLISCHUS, *They Wanted War* (New York: Reynal & Hitchcock, 1940).

A sober and reliable account of National Socialist Germany by an expert observer, the Berlin correspondent of the *New York Times* from 1933 to 1940. "The National Socialist aims that lie beyond the conquest of any individual country have been revealed to the world long since with a calculating frankness that won them the death-defying allegiance of German youth — a fact which precludes their abandonment — and seduced the rest of the world into not taking them seriously." See the review in *The Nation*, August 31, 1940.

WILLIAM D. BAYLES, *Caesars in Goose Step* (New York: Harper, 1940).

Revealing studies by an American newspaper correspondent of the leaders of present-day Germany and of their plans and intentions.

KARL LOEWENSTEIN, *Hitler's Germany* (New York: Macmillan, 1939).

The best brief survey of all aspects of the National Socialist government.

GUSTAV STOLPER, *German Economy, 1870–1940* (New York: Reynal & Hitchcock, 1940).

A survey of the tendencies of German economic policy, by one of the foremost experts in this field.

VERNON MACKENZIE, *Here Lies Goebbels!* (London: Michael Joseph, 1940).

The author is a professor of journalism in an American university. He subjects here the National Socialist propaganda in foreign countries to a searching analysis.

WILLIAM TEELING, *Know Thy Enemy* (London: Nicholson & Watson, 1939).

An analysis of the Third Reich as set against the background of German traditions.

ROTHAY REYNOLDS, *When Freedom Shrieked* (London: Gollancz, 1939).

Observations and reflections by an English newspaperman who had lived in Germany until the outbreak of the present war.

ERNST G. PREUSS, *The Canker of Germany* (London: Williams & Norgate, 1940).

This book, like two others by German émigrés — Rudolf Olden's *Is Germany a Hopeless Case?* (London: Allen & Unwin, 1940) and Sebastian Haffner's *Germany: Jekyll and Hyde* (London: Secker & Warburg, 1940) — tries to explain the events in Germany in the light of German history and psychology, and pleads for an understanding of and help for the "other Germany."

F. W. FOERSTER, *Europe and the German Question* (New York: Sheed and Ward, 1940).

An interpretation of German history by a German scholar. A book of fundamental importance which is worth a most careful perusal even if the reader should not agree with the point of view of the author in every detail.

LOUIS FISCHER, *Stalin and Hitler* (London: Penguin Books, 1940).

A well-reasoned and well-balanced statement by an American journalist who has lived many years in the Soviet Union.

VICTOR GOLLANCZ, *Where Are You Going?* (London: Gollancz, 1940).

In this open letter to Communists, a former sympathizer criticizes sharply the foreign policy of the Communists.

WILLIAM EBENSTEIN, *Fascist Italy* (New York: American Book Co., 1939).

The best brief discussion of all aspects of the development of Fascist Italy.

*   *   *

MARY A. NOURSE, *Kodo, the Way of the Emperor* (Indianapolis: Bobbs-Merrill Co., 1939).

A brief history of Japan, a people who, although accepting Chinese art and literature, refused to "accept the Chinese theory of an Emperor who ruled by virtue and could be dethroned by a revolution of the people if he failed to meet his moral responsibilities. Instead, the Japanese held to their traditional conception of an Emperor of divine descent who could do no wrong and to whom . . . the individual existed for the state."

D. C. HOLTOM, *The National Faith of Japan: A Study in Modern Shinto* (New York: Dutton, 1938).

A scholarly study of the development of the various aspects of Japanese official religion.

E. HERBERT NORMAN, *Japan's Emergence as a Modern State* (New York: Institute of Pacific Relations, 1940).

A scholarly study of the political and economic problems of the Meiji period, from Japanese sources. The continuity of Japanese policy is remarkable. In 1915, as the Allies were attempting to make China join the war, Japanese foreign minister Ishii expressed himself against the plan, "straightforwardly announcing that Japan could not regard with equanimity the organization of an efficient Chinese army . . . nor could she fail to regard with uneasiness a liberation of the economic activities of four hundred million people." (Seiji Hishida, *Japan Among the Great Powers*, New York: Longmans Green & Co., 1940, page 223.)

A. MORGAN YOUNG, *Imperial Japan, 1926–1938* (New York: William Morrow, 1938).

The author of this book has been for many years editor of one of the leading English language papers in Japan. He presents a firsthand study of the different movements which have agitated the critical years in Japanese post-war history.

ROBERT AURA SMITH, *Our Future in Asia* (New York: Viking, 1940).

A realistic and thoughtful appraisal of the Far Eastern situation and its effects upon the United States.

HARLEY FARNSWORTH MACNAIR, *The Real Conflict Between China and Japan* (University of Chicago Press, 1938).

An analysis of the opposing ideologies of Japan and China.

WESTEL W. WILLOUGHBY, *Japan's Case Examined* (Baltimore: Johns Hopkins Press, 1940).

A most scholarly and at the same time highly interesting treatment of the Far Eastern problem by a leading American authority on political science.

HALDORE HANSON, *Humane Endeavor* (New York: Farrar & Rinehart, 1939).

The story of the Chinese war, told by an eye-witness.

MEI-LING SUNG CHIANG, *This Is Our China* (New York: Harper, 1940).

EVANS FORDYCE CARLSON, *Twin Stars of China* (New York: Dodd Mead, 1940).

Both books, one by a Chinese author, the wife of the Chinese generalissimo, the other by an American officer, give a vivid description of the armies and of the people of Nationalist China in her struggle with Japan.

J. G. ANDERSON, *China Fights for the World* (London: Routledge, 1940).

A first-hand account of the Sino-Japanese war and its possible consequences.

FREDA UTLEY, *China at War* (New York: John Day, 1939).

The author, a British Socialist, tells of her experiences with the Chinese army and the Chinese people.

HALLETT ABEND, *Chaos in Asia* (New York: Ives Washburn, 1939).

A discussion of the situation in the Far East, by the *New York Times* correspondent in the Far East.

T. A. BISSON, *American Policy in the Far East, 1931–1940* (New York: Institute of Pacific Relations, 1939).

A brief and factual survey of the situation.

* * *

WILLIAM BULLITT, *Report to the American People* (Boston: Houghton Mifflin, 1940).

As ambassador to France, Mr. Bullitt had the opportunity to observe the disintegration of France and its causes from a vantage point. His appeal to the American people to awake and to face the situation courageously and intelligently is one of the most statesmanlike speeches delivered during this war.

WILLIAM ALLEN WHITE (ed.), *Defense for America* (New York: Macmillan, 1940).

Fourteen leading American citizens discuss in the volume with remarkable unanimity the necessary steps to safeguard the independence and democratic form of life of the United States.

H. N. BRAILSFORD, *From England to America: A Message* (New York: Whittlesey House, 1940).

The well-known English Socialist writer discusses in this small book the attitude of Americans toward the war. A book of the greatest importance and of cogent logic.

"SCIPIO," *A 100,000,000 Allies — If We Choose* (London: Gollancz, 1940).

The author pleads for the proclamation on the part of Britain of its war aims, appealing to anti-Fascists everywhere as definite allies, and implying a dynamic social and economic policy. In that connection, a novel by Douglas Brown and Christopher Serpell, *Loss of Eden* (London: Faber, 1940), may be mentioned, which in a very realistic way foretells in precise detail the possible results of "Pétainism," should Great Britain try to conclude a half-way peace.

WILLIAM S. SCHLAMM, *This Second War of Independence* (New York: Dutton, 1940).

This book draws conclusions from Europe's disintegration for the guidance of Americans.

JOSEPH ALSOP AND ROBERT KINTNER, *American White Paper* (New York: Simon & Schuster, 1939).

An understanding explanation of and plea for President Roosevelt's foreign policy, written by two Washington journalists.

RAYMOND LESLIE BUELL, *Isolated America* (New York: Knopf, 1940).

Although the book was written in the early stages of the war and based on the belief of the probability of German defeat, it contains many very worth-while considerations and suggestions.

CLARENCE K. STREIT, *Union Now* (New York: Harper, 1939).

This book, proposing a union of all the democratic nations to safeguard peace and to assure the growth of liberty, formed the starting point for the movement of the Inter-Democracy Federal Unionists, with headquarters at 10 East 40th Street, New York City.

ROBERT SHERWOOD, *There Shall Be No Night* (New York: Scribner, 1940).

The book edition of this play contains an important introduction by the author.

CHARLES G. FENWICK, *American Neutrality, Trial and Failure* (New York University Press, 1940).

A leading American authority on international law discusses the implications of the American neutrality legislation.

WHITNEY H. SHEPARDSON, *The United States in World Affairs* (New York: Harper, 1940).

An account of American foreign relations in the year 1939, in collaboration with William O. Scroggs. A most useful volume of documentary material.

HERBERT AGAR AND HELEN HILL, *Beyond German Victory* (New York: Reynal & Hitchcock, 1940).

Discusses the effects of a German victory on various aspects of American life. A book of great distinction. Written with vigor and clarity.

INDEX

INDEX

DATE DUE
